DIVAN
OF
JAHAN MALEK
KHATUN

DIVAN OF JAHAN MALEK KHATUN

Persia's Greatest Female Sufi Poet

Translation & Introduction
Paul Smith

NEW HUMANITY BOOKS

BOOK HEAVEN
Booksellers & Publishers

Copyright © Paul Smith 1986, 2005, 2012, 2014, 2018.

NEW HUMANITY BOOKS
BOOK HEAVEN
(Booksellers & Publishers for over 40 years)
47 Main Road Campbells Creek
Victoria 3451 Australia

www.newhumanitybooks.com

ISBN: 13: 978-1986622233

Poetry/Mysticism/Sufism/Women's Studies/
Middle East/Persian Poetry/Sufi Poetry

Many thanks to Rezvaneh Pashai
for all her help.

CONTENTS

7... INTRODUCTION

77... POETIC FORMS USED BY JAHAN MALEK KHATUN

87... SELECTED BIBLIOGRAPHY

*

89... PREFACE by Princess Jahan

93... A SELECTION OF *GHAZALS*

201... A SELECTION OF *RUBA'IS*

277... *TARJI BAND* (strophe poem)

287... ELEGY POEMS *(marsie)*

315... *QIT'AS* (fragments)

INTRODUCTION

Situated in south-west Iran, Shiraz in the 8th A.H. or 14th A.D. century, famous for its gardens, wine, poets and beautiful women, almost miraculously was spared the atrocities and genocide that the Mongols had committed in most of Persia in the previous century. The depth of depravity and cruelty of the Mongols towards the Persians has probably not been equaled in all of known history.

Some historians claim that Shiraz was built from the ruins of Persepolis, and others state that it was founded by the Arabs at the time of the Muslim conquest. Other traditions claim that Shiraz was built on the site of a city named Fars or *Pars* (which became the name for the province, *Parsa* becoming 'Persia') and was named after Fars who was the son of Masus, the son of Shem who was Noah's son.

Incidentally, Noah the great Spiritual Master, is known to have been a vintner and after his ark landed on the mountains of Ararat in the nearby land of the Turks he brought his family there and planted the grapevines he brought with him... some say he founded the city almost ten-thousand years ago and Shiraz has become famous for the grape that bears its name.

The three wise men or Zoroastrian Perfect Masters *(Qutubs or Magi)* are said to have set off from Shiraz to go to Bethlehem to recognize the Christ *(Rasool)*. Persepolis was built some 2500 years ago near Shiraz, dedicated to the Spiritual Master Zoroaster who settled near there some eight thousand years ago... although most scholars say 2600 years ago... but they confuse him with the last priest that bore his name.

Shiraz was a famously beautiful city, known for its variety of markets, being on the trade route from Europe to the Far East. All of the agricultural produce of Fars came to the capital, which was a bustling, lively city. The grains, vegetables, fish, fruit, honey and of course wine were known all over Persia and elsewhere. Each market and bazaar had its own specialty... and craft and art flourished in Shiraz before Jahan and Hafiz's time as it did then. The gold and silverware and the beautiful books with their fine miniatures were bought by rich patrons for their libraries and palaces from Shiraz's workshops.

During the time that Jahan and Hafiz lived there was a change in the art of miniature painting in Shiraz due to a new way of looking at the world that they and others brought about, that led to the great masterpieces that appeared later in Tabriz and Herat and elsewhere. Shiraz was also an important centre for the buying and selling of Persian carpets and cotton goods, cotton being grown in the valley. Because the city was a cosmopolitan centre on the silk-road many merchants passed through from the known world bringing not only merchandise but also news of distant, fascinating lands.

Shiraz and its outer villages were about twenty miles in circumference with a population of about 200,000 souls with the population in the central city behind the walls being nearly 60,000 and the area there about five miles in circumference. It was a cosmopolitan city with diverse peoples arriving constantly from all over the country and from foreign places. Shirazis spoke many languages apart from Persian: Turkish, Lori, Arabic, Hebrew.

Ibn Battuta the traveller from Tangiers, whose book *Rihla* or 'Travels' is now compared to that of Marco Polo... and who Jahan and Hafiz probably met, passed through Shiraz twice and described the city as follows… "Shiraz is a densely populated town, well built and admirably planned, well-known and has a high place among cities. It possesses pleasant gardens and far-reaching streams, fine streets and excellent markets. Each trade has its own bazaar. Its inhabitants are handsome and clean in their dress. In the whole East there is no city that approaches Damascus in beauty of bazaars, orchards and rivers and in the handsome figures of its inhabitants, but Shiraz. It is on a plain surrounded by gardens and orchards and intersected by five rivers, one of which is the stream known as Ruknabad, whose water is very sweet and excellent to drink, very cold in summer and warm in winter and gushes out of a fountain on the lower slope of a hill called al-Qulai'a. The principal mosque of Shiraz, which is called the 'old mosque' is one of the largest of mosques in area and most beautiful in construction. Its courtyard occupies a wide expanse paved with marble and is washed down every night during the summer heats. The leading inhabitants of the city assemble in this mosque every night and pray the sunset and night prayers in it. On its northern side is a gate leading to the fruit market which is one of the most admirable of bazaars and to which I for my part would give the preference over the bazaar of the Courier Gate at Damascus.

"The people of Shiraz are distinguished by piety, sound religion and purity of manners, especially the women. These wear boots and when out of doors are swathed in mantles and head-veils, so that no part of them is to be seen and they are noted for their charitable alms and their liberality. One of their strange customs is that they meet in the principal mosque every Monday, Thursday and Fridays to listen to the preacher, sometimes one or two thousand of them, carrying fans in their hands with which they fan themselves on account of the great heat. I have never seen in any land an assembly of women in such numbers."

Hamd Allah Mustaufi wrote in his book *Nuzhat al-Qulab* in 1340 about Shiraz as it was when Hafiz was twenty and Jahan was eighteen… "The city of Shiraz has seventeen quarters and nine gates… the city is extremely pleasant to live in but its streets are very filthy, hence it is impossible for any one to go about in these streets and not be defiled. The climate is temperate and here all trades may be followed. At most times sweet-smelling herbs are available and are sold in the market. The water is from underground channels called *qanats* and the best is from the conduit of Ruknabad… but the biggest *qanat* is called Qalat Bandar that runs under the tomb of the poet Sadi, which never needs repair. During the spring floods the rivers rush down from Mount Darak and passing outside the town flows off into Mahaluyah Lake. The crops are of medium produce and very often go up to famine prices. Of fruits, the grapes known as *mithqali* are excellent. The population are lean and brown-skinned; they are Sunnis of the Shafi'ite sect; some few being Hanafites and there are also Shi'ahs. Further there are many great *sayyids* of noble lineage here… who hold the Traditions of the Prophet and as traditionalists they are for the most part excellently esteemed. The people of Shiraz are much addicted to holy poverty and they are of strict orthodoxy… so that they are content to do but little trade. Hence there are many poor folk, though they refrain from begging, and do not fail to practice some means of livelihood… while the wealthy folk are mostly foreigners. Hence few Shirazis are very wealthy, and most of the people strive after good works and in piety and obedience to the Almighty have attained a high degree of godliness. Never is this city devoid of saintly persons, for which reason it was also called the Tower of Saints... but indeed, at the present day, it should rather be called the Robbers' Haunt by reason of the lack of justice and bold greediness that is too common here... The revenues of the city go to the Treasury, and at the present time they amount to 450,000 *dinars.*"

As for the previous seven hundred years Shiraz had been ruled over by non-Shirazis and in the past two hundred by those of Turkish or Mongol origin the population had accepted the idea that they were born to rule over them and the ruler of Shiraz, Mahmud Shah at this time, though not Turkish himself, had a Turkish wife Tashi Khatun (the mother of his youngest son, Abu Ishak, and close friend and a mentor of Princess Jahan) who was greatly loved and influential in her own right. She endowed many public buildings including a college... and often paid her respects at the tomb of the Spiritual Master Ibn Khafif known as Shaikh-e-Kabir who was credited with having brought Sufism to Shiraz four hundred years earlier.

Junaid Shirazi the poet and historian of Shiraz who died some months before Hafiz, wrote in his book on Shiraz about the shrines of the many Saints and Spiritual Masters who had graced this place with their presence and where Shirazis weekly or even daily went on pilgrimage. This was usually a surprisingly joyous and relaxed occasion with a picnic-like atmosphere and a chance to socialize with family and friends. There are many important pilgrimage shrines apart from that of Shaikh-e-Kabir that is in the northern Darb-e-Istakhr quarter.

An understanding of the multi-layered and interlocking and often conflicting structure of Shirazi society is essential to the understanding of the story of Shiraz at that time. On top was the ruler and although he was in power he usually did not directly control the everyday goings-on of the city. All of that was designated to officials such as the minister for police, tax-collectors, bazaar regulators, who were appointed by the prime minister. The prime-minister's life was often shortened if he antagonized in some way his master or if the king was deposed.

As the king and his prime-minister's power and responsibility usually covered much of Fars and not just Shiraz, it was necessary that the chief-judge become an important head of this ruling class who acted in the king's name but was also understood to be the representative of the ordinary citizen and thus was the bridge that could be crossed in either direction as in the life of Shiraz's much loved Majd al-Din who saved Shiraz on two occasions and like succeeding chief-judges were sent on important peace missions to other rulers by their kings. Even the nobles of the city would pay them daily visits to judge family matters. The ruler and the chief-judge could criticize each other but rarely did, as each was greatly dependant on the other.

The group that was most powerful and influential amongst the nobles were the fourteen hundred *sayyids* or descendants of the Prophet who received from the government yearly stipends. The Shirazi *sayyids* controlled much wealth in the city and did so by endowments of colleges and individuals and events. Such wealth and power also meant they were somewhat independent from the ruler and their ruler, their *naqib,* like the chief-judge wielded much power upwards and downwards.

Apart from the ruler, chief-judge and *naqib,* the various trade guilds leaders and neighbourhood groups were of much importance in how the city functioned. The king had to have the support of such organization's leaders or bosses who had the responsibility to keep order in the bazaars and seventeen quarters and if the city was under siege they oversaw the battlements and security of all the gates. These bosses tried to control the street ruffians, young so-called 'heroes' and gangs that were potential mobs that could be for or against the rulers.

Under these chiefs were the common workers who could easily join the mobs in the street if the occasion arose and the ruler was hated. Some were ridiculed by the nobles and called drunken rogues and reprobate-outsiders *(rindan)*, ruffians and no-hopers but such young men saw themselves as heroes *(pahlavan)*, and believed in the lore of chivalry and their groups welcomed and fed and housed strangers and gave protection to the weak and vulnerable when violent times befell the city. Hafiz and Jahan were always identifying themselves with the *rindan* but their *rindan* belief was more about an inner philosophy of rejection of the outer forms of hypocritical society and religious dogma and rituals and a freedom to reject reason in favour of love and divine-intoxication.

Apart from the chief-judges, leaders of the *sayyids* and the bosses of the guilds and neighbourhoods there was another group who wielded great power although they were not appointed by the ruler. These were the shaikhs and their families. The shaikhs were the head-preachers and Sufi leaders, such as the powerful black-magician Shaikh Ali Kolah who claimed he could control the *jinn,* and was a deep and dangerous thorn in Jahan's and Hafiz's sides for over thirty years.

Shiraz during the fourteenth century contained more than five hundred mosques and colleges *(madrassas)* and Sufi retreats and other religious foundations endowed by the aristocratic, wealthy, old, established families who were as a social group the most powerful and of whom the Baghnovi, Fali-Sirafi, Alavi-Mohhamadis. The famous chief-judge Majd al-Din who was revered by all Shirazis was from the Fali-Sirafi family. Most of Shiraz's religious establishment came from fifteen or more noble families.

Shiraz for some time had been under the benign administration of Mahmud Shah Inju, who was said to be a descendant of the Court poet and mystic Ansari of Herat. Mahmud Shah (Jahan's grandfather) was appointed by Amir Chupan Salduz the chief-commander of the ruler of all Persia, the son of the Mongol khan (king) Uljaitu who had ruled from the majestic capital he built called Sultaniyeh near Zanjan south-east of Tabriz and Sultan Abu Said succeeded his father Uljaitu in 1317 at the age of twelve.

Mahmud Shah was sent to Shiraz as the tax agent to administrator all the personal holdings of the sultan, and because of his mastership in this control of the finances of Fars he received a fortune for himself of an income each year of at least a million *dinars*. He had become independent and powerful in Fars with the exception of some of the mountains and plains of the province where robber bands still raped, murdered, looted and plundered.

As the years passed and the young sultan, Abu Said, became embroiled in a power struggle and intrigues at court, the taxes that were supposed to come from Shiraz (the second richest city in his kingdom) dwindled. Mahmud Shah seized the opportunity and used the taxes to protect the city by building many large brick-works with tall towers that were used as lookouts. The bricks of rammed-earth were baked then carried to rebuild the tall, thick wall that had been constructed over 300 years earlier that surrounded the city and was of 12,500 paces. He also cleared the moat that had been added at the turn of the century. He dropped some of the many taxes and helped the city's poor and the poets and artists and because of his generosity he and his family were greatly loved by the people. Mahmud Shah returned to Sultaniyeh, the newly built Mongol capital near Tabriz, and left the governorship of the province of Fars to his three oldest sons Masud Shah... (the father of Jahan), Kaikhosrau and Mohammad. His youngest son was the handsome and popular Abu Ishak (the same age as Hafiz) who would eventually succeed Masud Shah and become her and Hafiz's patron. Kaikhosrau, the second eldest son was put in charge of Shiraz in 1326 when Jahan was four and Hafiz six.

In 1334 Mahmud Shah and his oldest son Masud Shah... Jahan's father (who was at the time with him at Sultaniyeh) were relieved of their positions by Sultan Abu Said for supposedly enriching themselves and not passing on all the taxes to him. Sultan Abu Said replaced Mahmud Shah with Amir Muzaffar Inak, a Mongol officer. In fear of losing his wealth and power Mahmud Shah decided to kill his rival and with his followers chased him to the palace walls at Sultaniyeh wherein Amir Muzaffar sought refuge with the sultan. The palace was then attacked. Sultan Abu Said was enraged by this but Mahmud Shah's great friend the prime minister Ghiyath al-Din Rashadi intervened on his behalf and while many of the conspirators were executed Mahmud Shah was imprisoned in Tabarak castle in Isfahan and Masud Shah in Anatolia. The sultan soon sent Amir Muzaffar with many soldiers to take power in Shiraz and take hold of the treasury and all revenues... which amounted to 10,000 silver *dinars* a day. Amir Muzaffar was preparing to send to Sultan Abu Said what was left in the treasury but before he could do that Masud Shah's second oldest son and governor of Shiraz, Kaikhosrau, had him arrested and packed off with his men back to Tabriz.

After Amir Muzaffar's soldiers were ordered back to Sultaniyeh, Sultan Abu Said feared an invasion by the Khan Uzbeck of the Golden Horde... and that left Kaikhusrau in power until Masud Shah returned after being released from prison due to the influence of the sultan's prime minister and he was welcomed back by all Shirazis and a sullen Kaikhusrau, who was not liked by the population, had to allow his older brother to take the reins of power. Masud Shah decided after talking to his beloved step-mother Tashi Khatun and his brothers in Shiraz that it was probably a good time for him to go to Sultaniyeh and beg Abu Said to release his father still in prison in Isfahan.

He left his brother Mohammad in charge while he was away on his mission that all Shirazis prayed to be a success, as they loved his father dearly.

He finally found Sultan Abu Said on the battlefield with Sheikh Hussein, who greeted Masud Shah quite warmly. Masud Shah asked Sultan Abu Said for a note to allow him to go and procure his father's release. Abu Said talked with his advisors and returned and said, "That is impossible. But I offer *you* governor-ship of Shiraz and Fars like your father once possessed, but unlike him you must *pay* due homage to me... and I mean *pay*, not become a thief like your father became." Masud Shah replied, "Whatever my father did he did for the city of Shiraz, Fars and *all* of its people who he loves so dearly and not for himself... he always lived a simple life and believed in love and not hurting others. It seems to me from your problems at the moment and from rumours I hear about *your* prospects in the near future that there is no reason why I should pay any allegiance to you when I have the full support of my family and my people. Unless you release my beloved father I will return to my people and declare myself sole ruler and you can send another army to take Shiraz as before, but this time we will be ready for you... but I can't see you doing that in the foreseeable future. So, I must take my leave and bid you farewell… I do not think we will be meeting again." And with a slight bow he left and began the ride back, but on the way back he was talked into calling in on a friend at the court at Sultaniyeh. This friend told him that a little over a year ago Sultan Abu Said had a very interesting visitor, Mubariz al-Din Muhammad Muzaffar, the ruler of Yazd.

He, like his father, ruled from the fortress Maibad near Yazd. His father died some twenty-two years earlier and the thirteen-year old Mubariz took over and even at that age was said to be a fierce and brave warrior. He made Maibad his capital some four years later, ruling from a large fortress there. Around the same time the administrator of Yazd, Atabeg Yusuf Shah, was giving the king, Uljaytu, many headaches and Uljaytu confessed to his soon-to-be successor, his son Abu Said that he would like to find a way to get rid of him. So he invited Mubariz to his Court and gave him Yazd to placate him.

Mubariz secretly visited Sultan Abu Said and the adoring ruler conferred upon him the title of Amir Zada… 'birth by king'. Later the word leaked out that Kirman and Shiraz were mentioned by 'Amir Zada'.

When Masud Shah arrived home in Shiraz his treacherous brother Kaikhusrau, who had become addicted to power, convinced the soldiers that had remained at home to support him... and, when Masud Shah entered the castle he was arrested along with his brother Muhammad, and Kaikhusrau declared himself the new ruler.

At the end of November that year, 1335, Sultan Abu Said's wife, the famously beautiful Baghdad Khatun, went to him on the battlefield, slept with him and after they had sex she wiped his body with a towel impregnated with a deadly poison. It was rumoured she was jealous of the attention he was paying to her young, beautiful rival Dilshad Khatun. Afterwards Baghdad Khatun was murdered in her bath, the Greek slave named Lu'lu who had become a powerful amir, beat her to death with a club.

Arpa Khan, the nephew of Hulagu Khan the king before Uljaytu, Abu Said's father... after being appointed Sultan, sent an order from Sultaniyeh to Isfahan's prison to remove the head of Shiraz's beloved ex-ruler Mahmud Shah. A number of the amirs didn't approve of what Arpa did or of his ascension to the throne and they set up a rival sultan in

Musa, a true descendant of Hulagu... and not just of his brother. Musa promised that if he defeated Arpa in the coming battle he would allow the sons of Mahmud Shah to peacefully go to Tabriz and collect what was left of the body of their father and return it to Shiraz for a proper burial. Fearing the wrath of the Shirazis who loved his father and believed Masud Shah to be his rightful heir, Kaikhusrau allowed his brothers and his father's favourite wife, the much-loved and respected Tashi Khatun, to travel with him to collect the body and return it to the grieving population.

Two years later in 1337 Kaikhusrau made the mistake of executing the good friend and ex-minister of Masud Shah, the Amir Fakhr-ud-din Phirak, which was the last straw as far as Masud Shah and many others were concerned. Jahan's father, the rightful heir to the throne, disappeared down one of the *qanats* and escaped to Isfahan where that city's most powerful people were loyal to him... and where he assembled a sizable army to take back his beloved city. On returning and laying siege to the city the people rose up and some generals and a good number of soldiers left their posts and joined him. Kaikhusrau was soon captured and quickly executed.

Hafiz was then eighteen years old, small and ugly, and working in a drapery shop and studying at night when this occurred. His father who was a coal-merchant from Isfahan had died when he was seven and he and his mother who was from Kazerun were left destitute and were forced to go and live with his uncle, Sadi... who considered himself a poet like his famous namesake, Sadi of Shiraz, who had died about fifty years earlier and was still the most popular poet in the city. He and another Master Poet, Nizami, had greatly influenced the young man with such a remarkable memory that by the age of eight he had memorized the whole of the *Koran*... and Sadi's poems, and hence Shams-ud-din took Hafiz as his pen-name (one who knows the *Koran* by heart). He was determined to emulate his hero and had gained some notoriety with his poems in praise of the new king that he had read to mild applause in the various teahouses he frequented. These poems had come to the attention of the king's prime-minister, the wealthy and much-loved patron of the arts, Khwaja Haji Kivam... and so Hafiz received an invitation to read them at the gathering of poets *(musha'irah)* during the king's New Year's garden party... an event that

Masud Shah had decided to revive, being a lover of wine, music and poetry as was his father.

Also invited, along with many of Shiraz's esteemed poets was a new arrival in the city who had recently come from the upheavals in the court at Baghdad and had taken up a teaching post at one of the colleges, the thirty-eight year-old Obeyd Zakani.

Even today, nearly 700 years later, Obeyd Zakani is a controversial figure (some of his so-called 'obscene' works are still banned in Iran). But, he is considered Iran's greatest satirist, social commentator and a remarkable poet of profound mystical verse. When he arrived in Shiraz his reputation preceded him being the author of *Prodigies of Aphorism,* a compendium of wise sayings composed while at the court of Sultan Abu Said. He had been born in the village of Zakan near Qazvin and was of lineage connected to the Prophet. In Qazvin he held a teaching post then a judgeship but became disillusioned by the corruption and the class-structure in government of that city and eventually found his way to Sultan Abu Said's court where he gained some success as a poet and social commentator. But, on arrival in Shiraz he had found little interest in his serious writings and being a natural comic and satirist decided that the role of court-jester might be the way to get a finger into the royal purse-strings. He states in this *ruba'i*...

In arts and learning don't be clever like me:
or like me, by the 'great', hated you will be.
You want plaudits from such a time as this?
Musician, drunkard, or shameless beggar be!

And in another...

Sir, stay clear of knowing, if it happens that you stay,
or you will lose the pittance that you will get today;
play the fool and learn well the skills of... the fiddle,
upon great and small you can then... will-fully, play!

At this poetry gathering came together for probably the first time Iran's greatest mystical, lyric poet, Hafiz; its greatest satirist and social commentator, Obeyd Zakani, and its greatest female poet Princess Jahan. Jahan's father, Masud Shah proudly introduced into the gathering of Shiraz's most important poets his sixteen year old daughter who was petite and extraordinarily beautiful and already somewhat too liberated for the upper-class nobility that were shocked that this mere slip of a girl had the audacity to consider herself as a poet... a problem that she would encounter for the rest of her life as she states in her Preface to her large collection of poems, "I composed poems all day long. Sometimes untalented and lazy people teased or found fault with me. Only some people are able to compose poetry. If composing poems is so bad we wouldn't have so many poets. At first I thought it wasn't a good occupation because it was disapproved of and not liked in the society that I lived in. After sometime I realized that our Prophet Mohammed's daughter composed poems and other women too, including his wife Ayesha. I began to compose poems everyday... it became my pleasure."

Obeyd, who had a reputation already as having a roving eye for beautiful members of either sex (the younger the better) was immediately under her spell and began composing poems about her...

One more time... my head I'm losing:
with my heart, once more I'm playing.
She, is a princess... and I'm ordinary:
she, is a queen... and now I'm begging!
Lithe figure and long braid like a lasso:
queen of beauty, my heart she's ruling.
Her eyebrows are wide like a bent bow:

waist slim: dark, magical: she's lying!
A charming flirt, graceful and straight
like cypress: a juggler, she's cheating.
Without her, I have no light from sun:
no her... no purity in world I'm seeing.
Place where her ruby lips start to smile
sugar loses all of its value, I'm saying!
In my heart always, never from mind:
when with her... lovingly I'm talking.
Going to her is like going to a doctor:
relief for my aching heart I'm hoping.
Everyone complains about an enemy:
only of this friend... I'm complaining!
If Obeyd's eyes get a real look at her...
her from all calamities I'm protecting!

Princess Jahan was already quite proficient in composing the simple four-lined *ruba'i*, but it was the more complicated *ghazal* that fascinated her and which led her to ask her father to find her a teacher of this form that at the time was being sung at Court and in the markets and winehouses, the most popular compositions being those of Shiraz's Sadi and the great Nizami.

Obeyd would have offered his services in regard to teaching her this poetic form but it was the small and ugly young Hafiz that attracted her for this position, even though his *ghazals* at that time could not be compared to those of the much older poet and were in fact quite pedestrian copies of his hero, the great Sadi. With Hafiz there would be no romantic complications, both she and her father understood. He was hired on a small stipend with Masud Shah asking his chief advisor Khwaja Haji Kivam who had already seen a poet of promise and a remarkable 'memorizer' in the young Hafiz, to look after the details.

It would be two years before an event would occur that would make Hafiz and his eventually remarkable *ghazals* the talk of the city and lead to a friendship between the two young poets that would last all their lifetimes. But her relationship with Obeyd would be a strange and stormy one, often swerving between contempt and fascination and lust and jealousy. This *ruba'i* of Jahan's was probably about the later short time physical aspect of their relationship…

My loved one, calming my heart down is:
they all tell me that he… an ugly clown is.
He may not seem to be beautiful to others,

but to me he is and beside me lying down is.

Her father the king, Masud Shah, having recently experienced the treachery of his brother Kaikhosrau was ripe for even false rumours at his Court about possible seditious actions of his second youngest brother the hapless, but faithful Mohammad. He let his paranoia get the better of him and without telling Tashi Khatun, his father's wife who was the mother of his youngest brother Abu Ishak, and who was greatly revered by all the brothers and especially Jahan and all of the people of Shiraz as a loving, intelligent and saintly soul… he had his brother arrested in the dead of night and sent to prison in the castle-fortress at Safid. When news spread throughout Shiraz that this had happened his popularity took a sudden plunge but… after all, he was their king and perhaps his brother was up to something?

Fearing the growing power and ambitions of the fierce fighter and ruler of Yazd, Mubariz Muzaffar, he sent his youngest brother the handsome and brave and poetry-writing Abu Ishak to take some of the army to Yazd to 'persuade' Mubariz to agree to annex his holdings to that of the province of Fars and accept governorship under Masud Shah. After much bloody fighting and negotiations Mubariz signed an agreement to accept this, but as Abu Ishak informed his brother on return he was a most untrustworthy soul and a tough opponent of incredible strength and bravery.

After a little over a year of imprisonment in the fortress of Safid Masud Shah's brother, Mohammad, escaped and made his way to the camp of Pir Husain the Chupanid, known by all not only to be ambitious but quite ruthless. Possibly Pir Husain sent someone in there to free him, then he could march on Shiraz with a 'legitimate' heir to the throne and there were still many in Shiraz who felt Mohammad was terribly wronged by his brother. For two weeks in 1339 Masud Shah and the people of the city stood up to Pir Husain and his army even though his troops outnumbered them. After losing half his soldiers Masud Shah sent a message to Pir Husain and his brother Mohammad that at noon, in two hours, the gates would open and they could march into the city to the palace and that he would be gone. He escaped with a few guards and advisors down a tunnel that lead from the palace to one of the larger underground *qanats* that took them well beyond the outskirts of the city and to safety. Masud Shah's mother and his daughter Jahan decided to stay and hide out among the people. Masud Shah fled to Lauristan to find someone powerful to help him to try to take back Shiraz.

Within a month the hapless brother Mohammad was executed by Pir Husain and then he had the youngest brother Abu Ishak and his mother the much loved, courageous and beautiful Tashi Khatun dragged through the city to be then taken to Tabriz to be questioned about her husband's wealth and property. The people rose up, this being the final insult (after the senseless death of Mohammad) and freed them after she pleaded to the population in the name of her much-loved husband. Most likely Hafiz and Obeyd Zakani were involved in this revolution that eventually led to the populace attacking the palace and Pir Husain fleeing the city after losing many of his soldiers and much of his claimed booty. The Shirazis were a fighting and gallant people as will be often seen!

Pir Husain returned to help out his cousin Sheikh Hasan Kuchek defeat Hasan Borzorg in Tabriz who returned his help with an army to take back Shiraz and joining this army was that of the dangerous Mubariz Muzaffar of Yazd who now had eyes for the main prize, Shiraz... and the whole of Fars.

With Pir Husain gone Jahan's father Masud Shah simply marched back into Shiraz and resumed his ruler-ship. But his ease did not last long. On hearing of the size of the armies of Pir Husain and Mubariz that were heading for Shiraz he fled to Baghdad and took refuge with Hasan Borzorg! Chess has nothing to compare with the moves in this royal game!

The Shirazis fearing the vengeance of Pir Husain and the reputation of the ferocious Mubariz Muzaffar closed the gates and held out bravely against the huge armies for fifty days! Knowing they could not last much longer and their opponents had fared worse than they thought they would, the people called on their revered chief-judge Majd-al-Din Isma'il to leave the city and broker a peace with the invaders. This he wisely did to everyone's advantage gaining a promise from Pir Husain to overlook the city's previous relationship to him and to act kindly towards its people. Pir Husain rewarded Mubariz with the city of Kirman.

An uncomfortable but workable peace settled on the city by 1341. Hafiz was now working in a bakery at night and studying most days, and had learnt to get by with little sleep. He had become skilled in jurisprudence, had learnt all the sciences, including mathematics and astronomy. For many years he had been studying the great Persian poets and the lives and works of the Spiritual Masters. He was fluent in Arabic and Turkish. It is most likely that one of his teachers was Obeyd Zakani.

Early one morning at the bakery a worker who delivered the bread was sick, and Hafiz had to deliver to a certain quarter of Shiraz where the rich, ruling Turkish upper-class lived. Outside a mansion Hafiz's eyes fell upon the unveiled form of a young woman who was standing on a balcony. Her name was Shakh-e-Nabat... meaning 'Branch of Sugarcane'. Nabat's unique beauty immediately intoxicated Hafiz and he fell hopelessly in love with her and almost lost consciousness. He could not sleep or eat. He began to write *ghazals* inspired by her.

> *Lord, that bright candle lights night of whose dwelling?*
> *Our soul burns while asking: "That is whose darling?"*
> *That one overturns my heart and my faith and my religion.*
> *Whose bedmate, I want to know... with whom is living?*
> *May that lip of ruby wine be not far away... from my lip!*
> *It is wine of whose soul... giver of whose cup for drinking?*
> *Every one devises a spell for that one; but it is not known*
> *which way the tender heart goes; to whose magic-making?*

That undrunk ruby wine, has made me so drunk and mad;
it's whose companion and cup: with whom associating?
Lord, one so regal, face like the moon, forehead of Venus,
is whose peerless pearl... whose jewel beyond comparing?
Ask destiny of companionship of that candle of delight;
before God ask "That candle for which moth is burning?"
I said: "The insane heart of Hafiz burns without you!"
Hiding a smile, "For whom is he mad?" was the replying.

He heard she had been promised in marriage to Abu Ishak, the exiled (now ruling Isfahan with the help of Malek Ashraf, brother of Hasan Khucek and cousin of Pir Husain) handsome and talented youngest brother of Jahan's father, the exiled Masud Shah... and realized how hopeless was his love. Still, the vision of her beauty filled his heart and his thoughts were constantly with her. Then one day he remembered the famous 'promise of Baba Kuhi'. Baba Kuhi was a God-realized soul *(Qutub)* a Perfect Master-Poet who had died in Shiraz in 1050 and had been buried four miles from Shiraz on a hill named after him. Baba Kuhi had composed a *ruba'i* that had summed up Hafiz's position perfectly and gave him some hope...

Wherever a heart has blood flowing from it, I see it.

Crazy for hair of moon-faced ones? I admit I see it!
That particular Essence... the same in both worlds,
in moon-faced ones looks, pure, exquisite... I see it!

The promise that Baba Kuhi gave was that if anyone could stay awake for forty consecutive days at his tomb he would grant them the gift of poetry, immortality, and his heart's desire. Hafiz, interested in the third, vowed to do it, and... he'd had plenty of practice in not sleeping.

Every night Hafiz would go to work at the bakery then eat, walk past the house of Nabat, who had heard some poems of his in praise of her sung by the minstrel friend of Hafiz, Hajji Ahmed. One in particular had affected her...

To tell to you the condition of my heart is my desire:
to know news that your heart may impart is my desire.
Notice the desire so fundamental: the tale well known:
to conceal from the watchers spying art, is my desire.
'Night of Power' such as this that is precious and holy,
being with you until day sees night depart is my desire.
O no, that pearl that is unique, that is tender and lovely,
in the dark night to pierce, know every part, is my desire.
O breeze of the East, give some help to me in this night,
for to blossom when morning does start... is my desire.

For the sake of praising, to sweep the dust of the Path
with point from where my eyelashes dart, is my desire.
Like Hafiz, without regard for those who are censors,
verse beyond reason, loving, to impart… is my desire.

She had noticed him passing, each day more weary but with fire in his eyes that had lit the lamp of her heart for him. Hafiz was in a kind of trance. The only thing that kept him going was the love in his heart and his determination to keep the lonely vigil. On the fortieth day she ran out and threw herself in the dust at his feet, declaring she had lost her heart to him and no longer would marry Abu Ishak… but, he stumbled single-mindedly towards his quest. She remained in love with him for the rest of her life and was his Muse through whom he saw and praised God's Beauty in the most perfect of human form… the female form through which can be contemplated both the creative and the receptive nature of God.

The next evening Angel Gabriel appeared and gave Hafiz a cup containing the Water of Immortality and declared he had also received the gift of poetry. Gabriel asked him his heart's desire. Hafiz could not take his eyes off Gabriel. So great was the Angel's beauty he had forgotten Nabat. He thought: 'If Gabriel is so beautiful, how much more beautiful God must be.' "I want to be united with the Beauty of God!" he declared. Gabriel directed him to the perfume shop of Mahmud Attar who was the *Qutub,* the Head of the Spiritual Hierarchy at that time, the Perfect Master, who had sent Gabriel… and if Hafiz would serve him faithfully, Attar promised that one day he would attain his wish… but, he must learn to be patient and to obey him.

Hafiz joined the circle of Attar's disciples and on the Master's orders it wasn't until many years later, after Attar had dropped his physical form, that Hafiz revealed his Master's identity. Hafiz later married as Attar ordered him (not Nabat) and had a son.

Hafiz's vigil had made him known throughout Shiraz and the poetry he now created, in praise of his Beloved, and out of longing to gain his heart's new desire was soon sung throughout the city by the minstrels such as Hajji Ahmed and in far flung places. Jahan, loving Hafiz's 'inspired' *ghazals* now knew for certain that she had found her teacher and continued to received lessons from him which were paid for by Masud Shah's advisor the rich and wise Khwaja Haji

Kivam. All that was needed was the return of her father to power. She didn't have too long to wait.

A year later in 1342 Abu Ishak joined his army in Isfahan with Malek Ashraf's and on hearing of this Pir Husain decided to attack them there but he was beaten, and afraid of Mubariz Muzaffar, he decided to seek refuge with Hasan Kuchek his cousin, who immediately executed him. So much for family ties again!

On advancing on the now wide-open Shiraz, Abu Ishak convinced Malek Ashraf to let him enter the city first where the Shirazis embraced him and took up arms against Ashraf attacking his camp by night and sending his men packing. While this was happening, unbeknownst to Abu Ishak his remaining brother, Jahan's father Masud Shah had entered into a pact with a Chupani commander Amir Yaghibasti (Malek Ashraf's uncle!) and had entered Shiraz. Abu Ishak immediately yielded to the rightful claim of his older brother and left for Shabankareh.

Now was Jahan's chance to approach her father about re-appointing Hafiz as her poetry teacher. He agreed as did Hafiz who weekly went to the palace to give her lessons and their budding friendship began to bloom as did the interest in her of Obeyd and her in the crazy poet, joke-teller and unofficial Court jester. Hafiz complained in the following humorous poem while at Court to Masud Shah that he had been paid for the past three years by Khwaja Haji Kivam while Masud Shah was exiled but that now that he had finally returned and should take over paying him suddenly the money had dried up!

O monarch, just one, one with ocean hands, lion of heart!
You whose glory has many arts… to proclaim your estate!
All horizons were captured and all quarters were subdued
by happy reputation and fame of Masud Shah's state.
It could be an invisible voice has told you of my condition,
how my day that was radiant, became a dark night of late?
That which in three years I received from king and adviser,
in a moment was snatched away by the sky's mallet: fate.
Late last night while sleeping, in my imagination I saw…
at morn I happened to go secretly to king's stable's gate.
There, tied in the stall… my mule that kept eating barley:
pushed nosebag aside, said, "Do I know you?" as he ate.
I do not have any idea as to the explanation of this dream:
you interpret it, in comprehension near you none does rate!

But the situation was soon to change again! Yaghibasti, like Pir Husain before him couldn't bear sharing power and on a fateful day in 1342 as Masud Shah left his bath Yaghibasti had some of his men stab him to death. On hearing of this treachery Abu Ishak was soon to react. He contacted many of the nobles, guild-masters, gang bosses and neighborhood leaders who agreed to join forces with his men by opening the gates to them and attacking Yaghibasti in brawls that lasted in the streets of Shiraz for twenty days! Once again the Shirazis had been underestimated by a ruler. It is certain that Hafiz, Jahan who had left the palace on the death of her father and Obeyd all joined in the fighting. Soon the ruler of Kazeroun joined his forces with Abu Ishak's... Yaghibasti and his soldiers fled. Incredibly, a year later Yaghibasti and Malek Ashraf united their armies with Mubariz Muzaffar's and murdered and pillaged their way towards Shiraz, but... upon hearing of the death of the head of the Chupanid family, Hasan Kuchek, the two Chupanids stopped their advance and headed for Tabriz and possible power there and Mubariz, disappointed, returned to Yazd. So, in 1343 the talented, brave, handsome youngest brother, Abu Ishak, the son of the much-revered Tashi Khatun, the beloved step-mother of Jahan, to whom Nabat had been promised in marriage but whom she rejected (having fallen in love with Hafiz) now had undisputed power in Isfahan and Shiraz and would do so for most of the next ten amazing years.

During the reign of Pir Husain Jahan had renounced her status of royalty and had lived the life of an ordinary Shirazi and had loved the freedom and liberating effect on her as a woman of the upper class. She had frequented and drunk in many of the winehouses run by the Zoroastrians and Christians and was treated as an equal by the dozens of poets, minstrels and musicians of the city who performed there. They included the now-popular Hafiz, Obeyd, Haydar, Ruh Attar, Junaid Shirazi and a recent arrival from Baghdad and Yazd the famous Court poet Khuju Kirmani who soon, much to the chagrin of Obeyd became Abu Ishak's official Court poet, while Obeyd had to be content with being a jester again, who delivered satire, obscene jokes and an occasional mystical *ghazal*.

One of the greatest influences on Jahan at this time, and before this time, was the infamous female poet Mahsati who specialized in the *ruba'i* and lived in Ganja in the 12th century, during the time of the great Nizami. She was notorious for her liberated views and actions but especially for her 'obscene' *ruba'is* that also appealed to Obeyd who composed many of his own. She finally married a son of a preacher, the poet Taju'd-din Amir Ahmad whom she had (like Jahan would soon discover with her 'great love') found little satisfaction in their torrid relationship... and so she composed the following:

I'm Mahsati and I'm most fair of those to be had:
I am famous for my beauty, from Irak to Meshad.
Preacher's boy, you're nothing but useless... bad:
if I get no bread, meat or prick... I get really mad!

Here are some of Mahsati's non-obscene *ruba'is* that could easily have been composed by Jahan and obviously when one compares them to hers, they had a profound influence on her, as did the tragic life of the female poet of two hundred years earlier.

I am a drunk and of the drunkards... a slave:
I'm far from ascetics and of libertines a slave.
I'm of the moment winebringer comes saying,
"I can't, be free to join drinkers," I'm a slave.

Any one who desires a love that is full of grace…
at midnight in blood soaks prayermat, anyplace.
haven't you heard yet, lovers have pitched love's
tent beyond where seven heavens, turn in space!

Does night know anything about how lovers are suffering,
how from that goblet of calamity those lovers are sipping:
how grief will be killing them, if the secret they're hiding
and if it they're revealing, the people them will be killing?

A lover must go and risk one's life in love's way:
and turn upside down heart's peace every day!
When one witnesses that beloved is satisfied…
with suffering heart one dies, as one can't stay!

With your face your hair is in such harmony
I'm afraid I'll start blaspheming out of envy:
O graceful one, I will bow to that breeze that
from your face takes your hair… completely!

This body of mine has a heart full of ecstasy inside…
it also has soul with a thousand flames to see, inside.

And when day and night I am longing for your face...
I've two eyes full of streams flowing freely... inside!

All those nights that in love with you I slept... are gone!
You've left and what I told you must be kept... are gone!
You were soul's friend and you were my heart's peace...
you disappeared and those tears for I you wept are gone.

This affair of mine, beyond dry lips and wet eyes did pass:
your cruel arrow through my heart and soul flies, did pass.
To me, that fire of your love was like water in the shallows
but, when I stepped in to it, it then over my eyes did pass.

Abu Ishak re-appointed as chief minister the wise and wealthy and respected Khwaja Haji Kivam who soon made it clear to the young ruler that Hafiz's brilliance in Koran studies entitled him to teach the same at Kivam's college. Hafiz was summoned to Court and Abu Ishak was amused to see that the man who had won the heart of the most beautiful woman in Shiraz who had been promised to him was small and ugly, but he befriended him immediately... they had much in common, both knew the *Koran* by heart, both were poets and lovers of beauty.

Hafiz continued to teach Jahan who at the insistence of Tashi Khatun had returned to the palace. An example of how she would take a *ghazal* of Hafiz's then change it into one of her own can be observed by the following. First the *ghazal* by Hafiz (a much-loved and famous one)...

That lost Joseph will return again to Canaan: do not grieve;

sorrow's cell becomes a blooming rosegarden: do not grieve.

O sorrowful heart, your condition improves, don't despair,

this worried mind will rest peacefully again: do not grieve.

If springtime of life is once more upon the garden's throne,

night-singer, over head rose canopy's drawn: do not grieve.

If for a few days the revolving Sphere doesn't turn our way:

this wheel not always spins in one direction: do not grieve.

Do not be hopeless if you don't understand what is hidden,

a secret game is played behind the curtain... do not grieve.

When from longing for Kaaba you've set foot in the desert,

if you're wounded by the sharp Meccan thorn: do not grieve.

Heart, if the flood of death sweeps away all of life's foundation,

when in this torrent Noah is your Captain... do not grieve.

Although journey's stage is perilous and the goal is not seen,

each road will always end at the Destination: do not grieve.

Though we are separated from Beloved, troubled by enemy,

God causes and changes our every situation... do not grieve.

Hafiz, in your corner so poor, alone through dark nights...

while you are praying and reading the Koran: do not grieve.

Now, Jahan's *ghazal* that was influenced by the one above:

O my bewildered heart, from this world's sorrow, do not grieve:

world's condition goes up today, down tomorrow, do not grieve.

If this world's hurricane threw you into the blazing fire of love,

if your honour is upon the ground or even below: do not grieve.

And if you happen to live life like Jacob in the house of grief...

that lost Joseph will return again to Canaan, so do not grieve.

Every day seek and do not be hopeless about God's kindness,

people who have hope find what they hope for, O do not grieve!

If your aim is for the Kaaba do not turn off from desert's path, depend on this suffering, in thorn-bush don't go. Do not grieve!

Pain from that One's better than His healing: sit, be patient!

If you cannot find a way to heal heart's sorrow, do not grieve.

For in the world there is no trust... so might as well be happy:

water comes back to the dried-up river... and so do not grieve.

O gardener, best wait, be patient with this trouble with crows:

nightingale will return with a frenzied oratorio... do not grieve.

Jahan, how long do you want heart to suffer due to this world?

Your life settles down, if not today, tomorrow. Do not grieve!

Many of her poems from now on were about one who was to become really the first and great tragic love of her life... the newly appointed minister of Abu Ishak, a brilliant, handsome but vain and womanizing young man from

Jahrum, south-east of Shiraz, Amin al-Din Jahrumi. She was besotted by him and his long black hair from the moment he first appeared at Court.

My beloved, why in such a vile way keep treating me:
for God's sake tell me why do you treat me so badly?
Please do not be any worse to me any more than now:
I've lost all patience grieving over you, can't you see?
Our grief is killing us... don't let it exceed its bounds:
what is the full extent of the bounds of your cruelty?
I'm in love with your long, black hair falling in braids:
this deserves, that not broken is your promise to me.
I'll go off and start painting my face with my blood,
because... my beloved, you I can't find and can't see.
If someone other than me you happen to be choosing,
I'd still not find another but you to love... obviously.
I told the breeze of your lips and your beautiful hair...
because I want that breeze to bring your smell to me.
I didn't know that caught in the net of your black hair,
I... not being able to love anyone except you, would be.
Thank God that you keep staying in the world, Jahan,
sometimes you can help any poor beggar that you see.

Jahan's name means 'the world' and in many of her *ghazals* and other poems she uses a play on it or uses it as a double-meaning. This makes it difficult for her translators to know whether she is talking about herself or the world at large or both or the world of Jahan or a dozen other possibilities... but this is a part of her genius and playfulness. In the following *ghazal* she mentions how one of Hafiz's appeals to her in her desperate situation where she is being rejected and slandered...

Between Jahan, the world and all in it... is separation:
I am not in fear of my enemy or friend's consternation.
If I'm like a word in the peoples' mouth it isn't strange
because inside the shell is always the pearl's location.
To one who leaves the world with its good and bad...
the peoples praises or slander causes no perturbation.
"If you are simple and pure you will be seeing the Sun:
if the dark night is before you... have no trepidation."
I've placed this couplet by Hafiz in my poem because
this ghazal of his I love deeply... without reservation.
O my friend, I have no complaints about my enemies:
I only complain of friends... with enemy's disposition.
My temperament's garden's breeze is jealous, impure:

I hear it has ambergris scent from a heavenly station.
It could be likened to a bud the breeze easily blows...
and after being blown it's feeling joyful exhilaration.
Jahan, the world's beautiful but don't leave the grass:
place for enlightened ones waits near river's location.

The situation at Court with her displays of love-madness due to her fascination with the uninterested Amin al-Din began to create such a scandal that soon all of Shiraz was talking about her and singing her *ghazals* to him that she would openly read out or sing and dance to during the poetry gatherings that Abu Ishak would have every week where Obeyd would out of jealousy satirize her with his obscene verse and Hafiz, Khaju Kirmani and others try to take the attention away from her.

Tashi Khatun each day became more and more worried about the health of the mind and heart of her favourite step-daughter and finally went to her son to plead with him to talk to Amin al-Din to see if he could turn his eyes at least for awhile in Jahan's direction and away from his many conquests at Court and in the local whorehouses and winehouses. Abu Ishak eventually gave way to his mother's pleadings and convinced his young minister that a short affair with Jahan would put her out of her misery and stop this fascination with something forbidden and unreachable. Their affair commenced and Jahan was in ecstasy. Soon, (being in Jungian terms a 'animus-projector' or 'Don Juan' type) he tired of her and looked around for other hearts to break.

But Jahan was not one to be tossed aside so easily. She poured out her grief and bitterness at his rejection in *ghazals* and *ruba'is* that shocked her family and all at Court and had all of Shirazi high society talking about the young princess poet who did not seem to 'know her place'… but, the common people felt deeply for her and took her side as they would do for the rest of her life.

Loving you, has broken my heart wide apart…
to explain this any more is not within my art.
I'm always being teased by those opposing me:
I suffer more than usual and grief plays its part.
My family criticizes me, opponents even more:
but they, not my family, feel sorry for my heart!
This broken heart of mine leaves that one alone:
don't imagine he is faithful, for cruelty is his art.
In Jahan is no work, except burning in this love:

everyone in the world must play a grieving part.

I'm sure it would be better if I'd be like a drifter…

the world's King, Jahan, guards a drifter's heart.

She wanted him no matter what and she caused such a uproar that she had been cruelly abandoned and mistreated by him that she forced her uncle Abu Ishak into talking his unhappy young minister into marrying her, a woman he thought to be outrageous and to him a great embarrassment.

At this grand occasion at the palace all the local poets were of course invited and many read loving poems and minstrels like Hajji Ahmed sung *ghazals* to the young couple. Not so the envious and brave (and perhaps foolish) Obeyd Zakani who was still hopeful that she may have got over her infatuation and continue the affair she had once had with him. To the amazement and shock of all gathered there he recited this obscene *ruba'i* of his as his marriage present to her husband for all to hear, using a play on the double-meaning of her name as she often did, and joking about the petite Jahan in relation to the large minister…

Minister, the world (Jahan) an unfaithful prostitute, is not?

One of your stature, ashamed of such a prostitute... is not?

Go, find a pussy who to be fitting your size is quite able...

fit, for you, Lord of the world, Jahan... who is minute, is not.

It is said that Amin al-Din was greatly amused but not so Jahan or her uncle who had to wait for the laughter and obscene talk to die down before Obeyd received his rebuke. It would take years before Jahan could forgive her old lover for this offence.

At last Jahan was happy for a year or so but Amin al-Din wasn't and his answer to this was to continue to do what he was doing before they were wed. She let out her longing, grief and frustration in many hundreds of heart-wrenching *ghazals* and *ruba'is* that are unique in the depth of human desire and love and despair into which she sunk and gave expression to at Court in readings and song and dance, for she was said to have also been a fine singer and a wonderful dancer.

It must be understood that the upper-class and the royalty of Shiraz were of Turkish and Turkish mixed with Persian origin and hence the women were unveiled and mixed more freely with the males at that time and Jahan saw herself not only as a poet but also as a liberated individual... free of everything but the spell of her love for one who hardly ever saw her.

Many of her poems spoke of how she was laughed at by the nobles and how her husband was off with other woman and how her heart could not stop breaking. But, eventually something good came out of their relationship... she had a daughter, Soltan Bakht, the light of her eyes, whom she praised and mourned in many beautiful, heart-wrenching elegies after her death...

Although the world lied to kings and took their lives too...
kings of the world, Jahan, still desire the world... it's true!
Soltan Bakht's death has killed this world and me, Jahan:
heart of the world of Jahan is burnt up, this one can't undo.

(Notice again the clever play on her name and its meaning).

Hafiz had also married and had a child, a son, but still had a relationship of a platonic nature with his muse Nabat who never married for she had lost her heart to the small, ugly poet and rejected the king, Abu Ishak, who also eventually married and had a son, Ali Sahl, whose life like that of the son of Hafiz and the daughter of Jahan would be a tragic, and not a very long one.

Abu Ishak turned out to be an ambitious and often erratic ruler. Soon after gaining power he set his sights on Kirman and came into conflict again with his arch-foe the brave and brutal Mubariz Muzaffer of Yazd who was now ruling there. In 1345 and a year later he attempted unsuccessfully to take the city. Later in the decade he attacked Kirman again then Yazd but failed both times at a great cost, not only to the city coffers but to his own sanity. He seemed to be suffering from bipolar disorder and this led to bouts of terrible depression or exaggerated pleasure-seeking in wine and women and feasting. The parties at the palace became famous for their wildness and long duration and the false Sufis Shaikh Ali Kolah and the false ascetic Abdullah bin Jiri and their thousands of blue-robed followers began to denounce him and what they saw as Shiraz's lawlessness and contempt for 'Islamic ways'. He was too frightened to reign them in and they began to act like a religious police force against the *rinds* and open-minded poets and musicians and Hafiz, Jahan and Obeyd warned of their growing influence. They built a high tower in the city they hypocritically called 'The Tower of Unity' on which they could spy on the population. Shah Abu Ishak's paranoia extended to the people of Shiraz even though they had fought alongside him many times to rid the city of tyrants. He was afraid they would rise up against him and so prohibited the owning of arms except by his Isfahani soldiers and guards. The people began to resent him. His prime-minister Khwaja Haji Kivam tried to reason with him but insanely again he attacked Yazd and this was the last straw as far as Mubariz was concerned, noting that Abu Ishak had broken eight peace agreements with him. In 1352 from Kirman and Yazd the tyrant Mubariz brought troops together and marched on Shiraz where Abu Ishak was now drunk most of the time. The terrible siege of the city lasted six months and it was mainly the starving people that held off the dreaded foe. The neighbourhood chiefs and mob bosses were really the ones in charge of the defences and when Abu Ishak made the mistake of planning to execute one of them for something imagined, the district's boss out of self-preservation contacted Mubariz and opened a gate for his troops to enter.

During the siege Khwaja Haji Kivam died and at the end of it in 1353 Jahan's husband, Amin al-Din, fled through one of the *qanats* (underground water courses) with Abu Ishak who in his haste to escape left his small son Ali Sahl behind... who was eventually captured and cruelly put to death by Mubariz as was his wife and daughters, and as were many of Shiraz's courageous citizens. The raping, killing and pillaging lasted weeks. Obeyd's most famous poem *Cat and Mouse* is a parable about the battles between Mubariz (the cat) and Abu Ishak (the mouse).

When the cat saw the king of all of the mice
he boiled with anger, like a cauldron, bubbly!
Strong as a lion and kneeling upon one knee
with teeth he tore the threads and he was free!
He grabbed mice, smashed them into the earth
so that mixed with dirt, them you couldn't see!
The army of mice ran madly in one direction,
king of the mice ran in the other, haphazardly.
The elephant and the elephant rider had fled:
the treasure, crown, throne, palace no longer be!

Abu Ishak and his entourage fled to Isfahan where he began to gather a new army to take back the city but a year later Mubariz's sons laid seige to that city and he was brought back and executed in May 1356 in much style in front of Shiraz's leading citizens (Hafiz and Jahan would have witnessed it) on the steps of the main building at Persepolis. His final words were the following *ruba'i* (sadly, the only one that he is remembered for)...

No hope in family or stranger does remain,
the bird of life now has not a single grain...
all that we said throughout our life is gone,
nothing will survive us, but an echo, vain!

Looking back on the reign of Abu Ishak and the friendship of him and the wise Khwaja Haji Kivam years later Hafiz would compose the following...

I remember when dwelling in your street's vicinity was,
to my eye from dust of your door... gift of luminosity was.
From being with the pure I stood up like the lily and rose...
whatever was in your heart on my tongue in sincerity was.
When heart sought Divine Truths from old Man Wisdom,
Love was explaining... what for him a great difficulty was.
In my heart there was: "I will never be without the friend."
What can one do for all my heart's effort, only vanity was.
Last night, thinking of friends, I went to the Winehouse...
I saw winejar, blood in heart... foot in clay easy to see was.
I walked far and wide to find why separation's pain exists:

in this, without knowledge, reason's teacher certainly was.
In the end, truth about bright turquoise of Abu Ishak was:
it gleamed brightly... but helping him to pass quickly was.
It is a shame, all this tyranny, is in this place of ambush...
a shame, graceful generosity, in that high assembly... was.
Hafiz, you heard all the laughter of the strutting partridge:
he, of grasping claws of the falcon of Fate... carefree was.

As soon as the stern, strict religious fanatic Mubariz Muzaffar had entered the city Shaikh Ali Kolah and his followers had rushed to his side and offered their services in closing the winehouses and brothels and drug dens and policing Islamic law on the point of death. Obeyd fearing the worst and knowing he would be one of the first to be hunted down, having satirized Mubariz and often Ali Kolah, fled the city in the first week's confusion of murder and plunder.

I'm leaving the land of Shiraz as my life will be taken...
O, because of this unavoidable despair, heart is broken.
I go, beating head with my hands, feet sinking in shit:
what's to happen to me, on this road what will happen?
Now, I cry out like the nightingale that is lost in love...
now, like the heartsick bud, my collar's been torn open.
I leave this city I'm leaving what I have for an unknown

when I go through the city gate... my life it is gone then.

As I leave my Self, heart, friends, Shiraz behind me...

I go on, hopelessly looking back, remembering... when.

There is no strength in my hands left to hold the reins...

can legs go on when strength from them has been taken?

I'm so sick today and heart-aching from the pain of love:

no help wise friends, parents' advice I should've taken.

O Obeyd, this is not a journey that I wanted to make...

Sky pushes me, then the chain of Fate pulls me... again.

Hafiz laments the closing of the winehouses and takes a brave dig at Shaikh Ali Kolah in the following famous *ghazal* of his composed at this time...

O heart, the door of the Winehouse maybe they'll open;

perhaps the difficult knot of our difficulty... they'll open.

If because of selfish preachers they have closed the door,

for God's sake keep heart brave and happy: they'll open.

By the pure hearts of lovers drunk from the morning cup,

soon the door with love's prayer as the key they'll open.

Write a note of consolation to the daughter of the vine,

that lovers cry blood from grief and see... they'll open.

On the death of pure wine cut the strands of the harp;

it's tangled hair, young magicians quickly they'll open.

O God, they've closed Winehouse door; don't approve,

or the door of lies and deceit and hypocrisy they'll open.

Hafiz, this costume you wear, when tomorrow comes…

they'll tear away, and its cord you will see they'll open.

During the six-month siege Jahan with her daughter Soltan Bakht had hidden out, as before, with Hafiz and his friends. Mubariz, realizing she was the last of the Inju royalty and loved by the people used Ali Kolah's spies to discover her whereabouts and she and her daughter were locked up in the palace, a fate that would befall Jahan for most of the following twenty years of Muzaffar rule! Jahan would bravely complain about this and even threaten Mubariz in the following *ghazal…*

Listen, why to me do not you pay attention…

your prisoner please listen to! Pay attention!

Through the power you have you became rich:

such power made people to you pay attention.

If one day some Persian lady did take your life,

then you'll of crown, status too, pay attention?

You are the monarch now and you have power:

you can do anything, it is true? Pay attention…

don't let the world trick you and don't be proud:
life has its ups and downs, if you pay attention.
I put it all away... my heart, my life: I've ignored
it all in Mubariz's reign. Please do pay attention.
Jahan, in this world how much grief do you want?
You suffer much: to grief, you too pay attention.

And in this *ruba'i* she states precisely her circumstances under the reign of the Muzaffar's... Mubariz, and his more benign son Shah Shuja who succeeded him who on and off for almost twenty years kept her as a prisoner in the palace, only allowing her out to read her poetry and see her friends at certain gatherings, mostly at New Year.

I've nothing, no home, no heart, not a world
throughout this kingdom of the Muzaffars.
Don't be deceived, O Jahan, by this world...
one day's lucky, next unlucky, in this world!

A few years after their imprisonment her beloved daughter died in mysterious circumstances and Jahan let out her bitterness and grief in many heart-wrenching elegies.

O how I regret that I've lost my darling daughter...
my dear daughter's dead, so young when I lost her.
So kind... a face like the moon... but what can I do?

All patience I've lost... kept from her, as a prisoner.
now the nightingale's song isn't heard in a garden:
my beautiful girl cut from the garden, like a flower.
O heart, when will you go to the house where she is?
She left me: with the caravan has gone my daughter.
I cried out so loud even the sky heard my complaint:
tears ran deep... like rain down drainpipe they were.
She was always a girl who had a happy disposition:
why did she die? Did my bad luck transfer onto her?
Darling, Jahan's world was destroyed when you left:
you left a world and Jahan, when you so young were.
She took grief and happiness from the world, Jahan...
she passed away, now of world Jahan is relinquisher.
And in this *ruba'i*...

This misfortune of mine... God has given this to me:
O God, I do not wish anyone else has such a destiny.
Yes... I cannot stop weeping and I keep saying to all,
"O my companions... my Soltan Bakht is lost to me."

And around about this time Hafiz's son also died in what seems to be mysterious circumstances, possibly eating some poisoned food that was meant for his father, and Hafiz mourned him in the following *ghazal*...

A nightingale drank heart's blood and gained a rose:
the jealous wind's thorns struck the heart sharp blows.
The parrot was joyous from hoping for the sweet sugar,
but the torrent of decay tore away all hope that arose.
Forever your memory, my eyes freshness, heart's fruit!
You went so easily and now so hard for me it all goes.
Camel driver, my burden has fallen, a little more help:
relying on You, this journey was made with such woes.
Don't disregard my wet eyes or this my old dusty face;
this clay and straw hall of joy from azure sphere grows.
What a crying shame it is that the moon's envious eye
put my moon-browed in grave that the moon bestows.
Hafiz, you forgot 'king to castle' and missed your move!
What to do? Time tricks again. I am careless, I suppose.

Mubariz's son Shah Shuja who had taken control by blinding and imprisoning his father who cut off the heads of hundreds while holding the *Koran* in one hand and his sword in the other was a liberated ruler in the style of Abu Ishak. He loved poetry and was a fine poet and immediately opened the winehouses and drew poets to his Court from all over Fars. But even the requests of Hafiz and other Shirazi poets to free the tragic and mourning Princess Jahan fell on deaf ears with him for like his father he knew that she may become the focal point of unrest if she was returned to the people who loved her so much. But, under his rule that continued for most of the years from 1358 until 1384 (his brutal Mubariz-like brother Shah Mahmud deposed him for two years, 1364-6) he allowed her to appear at more functions in the palace to recite her poems and occasionally converse with her friends and in particular her mentor, Hafiz.

For many of these years she kept expecting the return of her long-disappeared husband Amin ad-Din to free her and she composed hundreds of *ghazals* pleading for him to come back to her but eventually this fascination and desire for him faded and this desire was replaced by a deep longing for a new beloved... the Divine Beloved or the Perfect Master as can be seen in many of the poems composed in the later years of her life that more and more reflected the point of view of the spiritual *rind* or outsider or the dervish.

O God, please give my afflicted heart some good news...
and do something so those I love... me again will choose.
Take notice of my spiritual views and also of my religion,
victory to my enemies, strangers, friends: nothing to lose!
Heal me with happiness because I am tired of suffering...

make one worthless worthy with Your grace: me peruse!
We cannot find our way without a leader who is wise...
those following be impressed that to follow You I choose.
Shed light, show pleasantly candle of the deceased's face:
to heart's melancholic bird give plumage that will enthuse.
When arrows of an evil event are shot by Fortune's bow...
give my heart and my soul a shield... so that I cannot lose!
On Resurrection Day You forgive sins because of prayers:
forgive all my sins from my cries at dawn, if You choose.

Like Obeyd (who wrote 'obscene' parodies of the Sufis such as his infamous 'Book of Masturbation' and Hafiz who criticized the 'hypocritical wearers of blue robes') she seemed to reject the role of the 'Sufi' perhaps because of the continuing presence of false Sufi masters like Shaikh Ali Kolah and his many blue-robed followers who continued to make the lives of the more open-minded Shirazis most difficult.

Early on she would compose this witty *ruba'i*...
I swore that him again I would never see:
deaf to temptations of sin... I'd be a Sufi!
Then I knew that it wasn't in my nature...
renunciations are now renounced, by me!

Hafiz was self-exiled for a number of years in Isfahan in the late 1360's because of the false rumours and threats of Shaikh Ali Kolah and certain members of the clergy whom he had openly criticized and Obeyd was unable to return to Shiraz until he was finally invited back by an intrigued Shah Shuja... but Obeyd's sense of humour and honesty rubbed even open-minded Shah Shuja the wrong way and he died in abject poverty in 1373 having one last blast at the doctor who attended him on his deathbed...

To this stupid doctor no one should apply
to be treated... if one doesn't want to die.
Finally the angel of death to him will say:
"That which you sold for years, now buy!"

Eleven years later with the death of Shah Shuja in 1384 she was released at the age of sixty from her prison in the palace and was able to live once again with her friends, Hafiz and the minstrels and the ordinary people of Shiraz who saw her like Hafiz as one of their champions who had suffered much like he had to help liberate their hearts and minds and the city they all loved so much. We do know that by this time the perfect Master Mahmud Attar had passed his mantle of God-realization on to Hafiz and it is most likely that she became one of Hafiz's followers in the spiritual sense from that time and one of his inner circle. Perhaps many of her poems of this later date were written to him in his state of being the Beloved.

It is not worth asking for even one favour from anybody…
You alone in this world give daily bread to anyone like me.
When I came into the world I realized no one is oneself…
it is only the kindness of Yours that rescued us, obviously!
No one finds the right way if one asks an unworthy one…
separate the Friend's way, from that of anyone unworthy.
In all this world there is not one anything similar to You:
come to our rescue with Your grace… and please help me!
In this boundless sea of Yours I am such a small thorn…
and a small thorn can never be found upon top of the sea.

I have read a few reports that during this period Hafiz (who had lost his wife some years earlier) and Jahan married, but while I think this is possible I believe it is more likely that after she left the palace she went and lived with Hafiz… (possibly they married to avoid prying eyes and further controversy).

Hafiz dropped his physical form in 1392 and it is said that she survived him by many years, eventually collecting all her many poems together into a *Divan* and writing her unique Preface to it. Perhaps Hafiz did give her illumination before he passed on, for she was able to state at the end of her life, after all the suffering and loneliness she went through...

Is there a kind of kindness God has withheld from me?
If I could, in a thousand languages I'd be appreciative!
I remember that One in my heart, every day and night;
if I didn't I would hate it, leave it and it... not forgive!
When I'm looking at everything, I'm seeing only God:
my greatest wish is for whatever God, will me... give!

Poetic Forms Used by Jahan Malek Khatun

The *Ghazal*.

There is really no equivalent to the *ghazal* (pronounced *guz'el*) in English poetry although Masud Farzaad,* perhaps the greatest Iranian authority on Hafiz (he spent much his lifetime finding the Variorum Edition) and his *ghazals* says, the sonnet is probably the closest. As a matter of fact, the *ghazal* is a unique form and its origin has been argued about for many centuries.

Some say that the *ghazal* originated in songs that were composed in Persia to be sung at court before Persia was converted to Islam, but not one song has survived to prove this. It is also possible that originally the *ghazals* were songs of love that were sung by minstrels in the early days of Persian history and that this form passed into poetry down the ages. I find this explanation plausible for the following reasons: firstly, the word *ghazal* means 'a conversation between lovers.' Secondly, the *ghazals* of Hafiz, Sadi and others were often put to music and became songs, which have been popular in Persia from ancient times until now.

Other scholars see the *ghazal* as coming from Arabic poetry, especially the prelude to longer poems: they say that this prelude was isolated and changed, to eventually become the *ghazal*. The Arabic root of the word *ghazal* is *gazl* which means: spinning, spun, thread, twist... the form of the *ghazal* is a spiral.

Whatever the origin, by the fourteenth century the *ghazal* had become a mature form of poetry. Among the great *ghazal* writers in Persian of the past were Nizami, Farid ad-Din 'Attar, Rumi and Sadi; but with the *ghazals* of Hafiz and other poets in Shiraz including Jahan during his lifetime this form reached its summit.

The form of the *ghazal* at first glance seems simple, but on a deeper inspection it will be found that there is more to it than one at first sees.

It is usually between five and fifteen couplets *(beyts* or 'houses')*, but sometimes more. A *beyt* is 'a line of verse split into two equal parts scanning exactly alike.' Each couplet has a fixed rhyme which appears at the end of the second line. In the first couplet which is called the *matla* meaning 'orient' or 'rising,' the rhyme appears at the end of both lines. This first couplet has the function of 'setting the stage' or stating the subject matter and feeling of the poem. The other couplets or *beyts* have other names depending on their positions. One could say that the opening couplet is the subject, the following couplets the actions: changing, viewed from different angles, progressing from one point to another, larger and deeper, until the objective of the poem is reached in the last couplet. The final couplet is known as the *maqta* or 'point of section.' This couplet or the one before it almost always contains the *takhallus* or pen-name of the poet, signifying that it was written by him and also allowing him the chance to detach himself from himself and comment on what effect the actions of the subject matter in the preceding couplets had on him. Often the poet uses a play on words when he uses his own pen-name... ('Hafiz' for example, means: a preserver, a guardian, rememberer, watchman, one who knows the *Koran* by heart. 'Jahan' means: the world).

In the *ghazal* the Persian Master Poets found the ideal instrument to express the great tension between the opposites that exist in this world. Having the strict rhyming structure of the same rhyme at the end of the second line of each couplet (after the first couplet) the mind must continually come back to the world and the poem and the rhyme. But by being allowed to use any word at the end of the first line of each couplet, one can be as spontaneous as possible and give the heart its full rein. This of course happens also in the first line of the first couplet, for whatever word or rhyme-sound that comes out in the first line sets the rhyme for the rest of the *ghazal*. So the 'feeling' created by the rhyme is one that comes spontaneously from the heart, and this spontaneity is allowed to be expanded from then on in the non-rhyming lines, and to contract in those lines that rhyme, when the mind must function as an 'orderer' of the poem. This expansion and contraction, feeling and thinking, heart and mind, combine to produce great tension and power that spirals inward and outward and creates an atmosphere that I would define as 'deep nostalgia.' This deep nostalgia is a primal moving force that flows through all life, art and song, and produces within whoever comes into contact with it when it is consciously expressed, an irresistible yearning to unite the opposites that it contains. In the *ghazal* any metre can be employed except the *ruba'i* metre.

The true meaning of Sufism, apart from the recognition of God in human form as the *Qutub* or the *Rasool* or the Christ is *tassawuf*... which means to get to the essence of everything. Adam was the first poet and it is said that he named everything and invented the first alphabet from which all others come. But Adam was not only the creator of conscious language as we know it, he was also the creator of song and the perfect form through which he created songs in praise of Eve his true Beloved, her beauty was displayed in the spiral form of the *ghazal*. So, the *ghazals* he composed and sung to her before their eventual Spiritual Union were of longing and separation and those after... of the bliss of Union. He used the same form of song about other events including the great sorrow and deep nostalgia about the loss of his favourite son Abel.

Two of Arabia's most careful and serious historians Tabari (d.923) and Masudi (d.957) state that the first poem ever composed in known history was one by Adam on the death of Abel and the form was the *ghazal*.

The lands are changed and all those who live upon them,
the face of the earth is torn and surrounded with gloom;
everything that was lovely and fragrant has now faded,
from that beautiful face has vanished the joyful bloom.
What deep regrets for my dear son... O regrets for Abel,
a victim of murder... who has been placed into the tomb!

Is it possible to rest, while that Devil that was cursed
who never fails or dies… up from behind us does loom?
"Give up these lands and all of those who live on them;
I was the one who forced you out of Paradise, your room,
where you and your wife were so secure and established,
where your heart did not know of the world's dark doom!
But you, you did escape all of my traps and my trickery,
until that great gift of life… upon which you did presume
you went and lost… and from Aden the blasts of wind,
but for God's Grace, would've swept you like a broom!"

It is said that thousands of years after Adam, the Perfect Spiritual Master Noah, settled Shiraz after his ark landed in the Turkish lands on the mountains of Ararat and was a vintner who brought the first vines that he carried with him was also a poet who composed in this form as did the *Qutub* of some three thousand years later who also settled his people he had led from their homeland in Bactria (northern Afghanistan) to Fars (Persia)… Zoroaster.

His *gathas* or hymns are in rhyme-structure the first two couplets of the *ghazal* that would later be known as the *ruba'i*. And so the *ghazals* of the Zoroastrians were sung in their winehouses and fire temples throughout our land until the Muslim Arabs invaded and converted most to Islam, but poets and minstrels would not give up their much loved eternal God-given *ghazal* or the wine of Noah as well, which had its distant progeny in the *mesqali* grape.

The clandestine winehouses run by the Zoroastrians and Christians became the venues for many hundreds of years of the *ghazal*. In these winehouses Persians could criticize their Arab and Turkish rulers and their police chiefs and false Sufi masters and hypocritical clergy who censored and forbade them to practice the drinking of wine and the appreciation of beautiful faces and forms of unveiled women and handsome young men. In the winehouses the truth could be told and this truth was quickly spread by the minstrels in the market places and even at court through what was becoming a popular form of expression amongst the masses. And although in fact the actual drinking of wine finally became less because of the religious restrictions, it as a symbol of truth, love and freedom became more widespread.

Of course there always existed another 'Winehouse' where the Wine of Divine Love and Grace was poured out by the Winebringer or *Qutub,* the Perfect Master or the Old Magian. Here the wine and truth that flowed freely from heart to heart was of the spiritual nature and made the lover or drunkard so intoxicated with the Divine Beloved that he became *mast*-like... mad with longing to be united with the Eternal One, Whose beauty he saw and appreciated in the face and form and personality of his earthly beloved whom he praised, wooed, begged, cajoled, described, desired and desperately longed for through his *ghazals* and by his actions and with each breath of his whole life he came closer to the Eternal Beloved. Human love became transmuted into Divine Love. Hafiz's love for Shakh-e Nabat is an example of this.

Although the poets of the *ghazal* may appear to many as open-minded, drunken, outcast lovers, it does not necessarily mean that they all drank the juice of the grape... for it is an inner state that they often were expressing. The *ghazal* is a conversation between the lover and the beloved and as in all intimate conversation... the talk flows both ways. The subject may not necessary be about love, but it is always from the point of view of one who loves truth, love and beauty.

*Hafeez and his Poems by Masud Farzaad. Stephen Austin & Sons Ltd. Hertford, 1949.

The *Ruba'i*

Many scholars of Persian Poetry believe that the *ruba'i* is the most ancient Persian poetic form that is original to this language and they state that all other classical forms including the *ghazal, qasida, masnavi, qit'a* and others originated in Arabic literature and the metres employed in them were in Arabic poetry in the beginning… this, can be disputed.

The Persian language is a fine intercourse of Arabic (a masculine-sounding language) and Pahlavi (feminine-sounding language) that is mainly a descendant of the profound language of the Spiritual Master Zoroaster… Zend. Sanskrit is also a branch of that ancient language* (e.g. Zend: *garema* or heat is in Sanskrit *gharma,* in Pahlavi is *garma,* Persian… *garm)* given to us by that prophet whose perfect and profound teachings in the *gathas* of the *Avesta* were composed in a form very close to the *ruba'i* which one might believe could give him the title not only of the founder of the Persian language and people and mysticism… but also of Persian poetry's most individualistic form of poetic expression.

One can trace the origins of this poetical language back almost 7000 years to Zoroaster's time, not merely less than 2600 years... a mistake that most recent scholars made by confusing the last Zoroastian *priest* bearing his name with that of this original Prophet, the *Rasool* or Messiah, who like Moses, led out his people from their original Aryan lands in Bactria, when they were invaded by many hordes of murderous barbarians.

On that remarkable and in many aspects, far-reaching journey, an argument occurred amongst his people when they had reached what we today call India and many left him and settled there and their language eventually evolved into Sanskrit. Zoroaster then took his remaining followers west and finally settled near Shiraz in Fars, and Zend eventually became Pahlavi and the Aryan language continued west and founded many languages in Europe, including English.

Now as to the origin of the metre of the *ruba'i* I offer two of Zoroaster's poems or *gathas* to enjoy and consider, even though the metre may not be that of the *ruba'i*, the rhyme structure and content are similar.

Wise One, with these short poems I come before You,
praising Your Righteousness, deeds of Good Mind too.

And when I arrive at that bliss that has come to me...
may these poems of this man of insight... come through.
And another...
May good rulers and not evil ones over us be ruling!
O devoted, by doing good works for mankind, bring
rebirth... prepare all this for what's good for all men:
through work in the field, let ox for us be fattening.

The *ruba'i* is a poem of four lines in which usually the first, second and fourth lines rhyme and sometimes with the *radif* (refrain) after the rhyme words... sometimes all four rhyme. It is composed in metres called *ruba'i* metres. Each *ruba'i* is a separate poem in itself and should not be regarded as a part of a long poem as was created by FitzGerald when he translated those he attributed to Omar Khayyam.

The *ruba'i* (as its name implies) is two couplets *(beyts)* in length, or four lines *(misra)*. The *ruba'i* is a different metre from those used in Arabic poetry that preceded it.

How was this metre invented? The accepted story of Rudaki (d. 941) creating this new *metre* of the *hazaj* group which is essential to the *ruba'i* is as follows: one New Year's Festival *(Nowruz)* he happened to be strolling in a garden where some children played with nuts and one threw a walnut along a groove in a stick and it jumped out then rolled back again creating a sound and the children shouted with delight in imitation, 'Ghaltan ghaltan hami ravad ta bun-i gau,' (Ball, ball, surprising hills to end of a brave try). Rudaki immediately recognised in the line's metre a new invention and by the repetition four times of the *rhyme* he had quickly created the *ruba'i*... and is considered the first master of this form and the father of classical Persian Poetry.

Shams-e Qais writing two hundred years later about this moment of poetic history and the effect of this new form on the population said the following... "This new poetic form fascinated all classes, rich and poor, ascetic and drunken rebel-outsider(rend), all wanted to participate in it... the sinful and the good both loved it; those who were so ignorant they couldn't make out the difference between poetry and prose began to dance to it; those with dead hearts who couldn't tell the difference between a donkey braying and reed's wailing and were a thousand miles away from listening to a lute's strumming, offered up their souls for a *ruba'i*. Many young cloistered girls, from passion for the song of a *ruba'i* broke down the doors and their chastity's walls; many matrons from love for a *ruba'i* let loose the braids of their self-restraint."

And so, the *ruba'i* should be eloquent, spontaneous and ingenious. In the *ruba'i* the first three lines serve as an introduction to the fourth that should be sublime, subtle or pithy and clever. As can be seen from the quote by Shams-e Qais above, the *ruba'i* immediately appealed to all levels of society and has done so ever since. The nobility and royalty enjoyed those in praise of them and the commoner enjoyed the short, simple homilies... the ascetic and mystic could think upon epigrams of deep religious fervour and wisdom; the reprobates enjoyed the subtle and amusing satires and obscenities... and for everyone, especially the cloistered girls and old maids, many erotic and beautiful love poems to satisfy any passionate heart.

Almost every major and minor poet in Persia composed at some time in the *ruba'i* form.

---

*Note: See 'Comparative Grammar, Lecture 6' in 'Lectures on the Science of Language' 1861 By Max Muller, Reprint Munshi Ram Manohar Lal, Delhi, 1965.
The Encyclopaedia Britannica Volume xxi, Eleventh Edition Cambridge 1911 (Pages 246-8).

The *Qit'a*

The *qit'a* or 'fragment' must consist of at least two couplets and is similar to a *ghazal* or a *qasida* with the second lines of the couplets all having the same rhyme... but in the first couplet the double-rhyme does not usually appear. It can be composed in any metre except for that of the *ruba'i*. It can be a fragment from a *qasida* or a *ghazal*, or it may be complete in itself. Hafiz and others often used this form to write obituaries on people whom he knew as did many other poets.

The *Tarji-band*

This kind of strophe (band) poem consists of a series of stanzas each containing a variable but equal, or nearly equal, number of couplets all in one rhyme, these stanzas being separated from each other by a series of isolated couplets that mark the end of each strophe. If the same couplet (or refrain) is repeated at the end of each *band*, or strophe, the poem is a *tarji-band*, or 'return-tie'.

SELECTED BIBLIOGRAPHY

THE COMPLETE DIVAN OF JAHAN KHATUN. Edited by Dr. Poor Andokht Kashani Rad and Dr. Kamel Ahmad Nejad. Sherkate Ghalam. 1994. (The numbers in this translation of the *ghazals* are the same as in this edition.)

THE BOOK OF JAHAN KHATUN Translation by Paul Smith & Rezvaneh Pashai, Introduction by Paul Smith, New Humanity Books, 2016.

PRINCESSES, SUFIS, DERVISHES, MARTYRS & FEMINISTS: TEN GREAT WOMEN POETS OF THE EAST. A Selection of the Poetry of Rabi'a of Basra, Rabi'a Balkh, Mahsati, Lalla Ded, Jahan Khatun, Makhfi, Hayati, Tahirah and Parvin. Introduction & Translations by Paul Smith, New Humanity Books, Campbells Creek 2016.

RUBA'IYAT OF JAHAN KHATUN, Translation by Paul Smith & Rezvaneh Pashai, Introduction by Paul Smith, New Humanity Books, 2012.

HAFIZ OF SHIRAZ by Paul Smith. 3 vols. (Jahan is one of the six main characters in this 1900 page 3 vol. novel-biography). New Humanity Books, Campbells Creek. 2000-10.

THE POETS OF SHIRAZ, Translation & Introduction by Paul Smith, New Humanity Books, 2012.

DIVAN OF HAFIZ. Translation & Introduction by Paul Smith. 2 vols. New Humanity Books. 1986. Revised paperback New Humanity Books 2005, 2012.

MAST-HAFIZ (GOD-DRUNK HAFIZ). Rokneddin Homayoun Farrokh. 8 vols. Saatar Publications 1975. (An enormous, important source on Hafiz, Jahan, Obeyd and their time in Shiraz and Fars).

SHIRAZ IN THE AGE OF HAFEZ. The Glory of a Medieval City. John Limbert. University of Washington Press. 2004.

SHIRAZ. Persian City of Saints and Poets. Arthur J. Arberry. University of Oaklahoma Press. 1960.

A LITERARY HISTORY OF PERSIA. Edward G. Browne. 4 vols. Cambridge University Press. 1920.

THREE POETS OF SHIRAZ: Hafez, Obeyd Zakani and Jahan Khatun. Dick Davis. Mage Publishers. Forthcoming.

PIERCING PEARLS: THE COMPLETE ANTHOLOGY OF PERSIAN POETRY (2 Vols.) Translations, Introduction & Notes by Paul Smith New Humanity Books 2011.

BORROWED WARE. Medieval Persian Epigrams. Trans. Dick Davis. Mage Pub. 1997. (One Jahan poem).

THE TRAVELS OF IBN BATTUTA. (RIHLA) 3 vols. Translated by H.A.R. Gibb. Cambridge U. Press. 1958.

SUPPRESSED PERSIAN. An Anthology of Forbidden Literature. Translated with Notes and an Introduction by Paul Sprachman. Mazda Publications. 1995. (Chapters on Obeyd and Mahsati.)

THE COMIC WORKS OF UBAYD-I ZAKANI: A Study of Medieval Persian Bawdy, Verbal Aggression and Satire by Paul R. Sprachman. University of Chicago Degree Dissertation. 1981.

THE ETHICS OF THE ARISTOCRATS AND OTHER SATIRICAL STORIES. Obeyd-e Zakani. Translated by Hasan Javadi. Jahan Book Co. 1985.

OBEYD ZAKANI: THE DERVISH FOOL. A Selection of His Poetry, Prose, Satire, Jokes & Ribaldry. Translation and Introduction by Paul Smith. New Humanity Books 2005, 12.

OBEYD ZAKANI'S POETICAL WORKS. Editors: Abbas Eghbal and Parviz Atabaki. Bonyade Nashre Kitab.

LAYLA & MAJNUN by Nizami. Translation and Introduction by Paul Smith. New Humanity Books 2005, 10.

THE TREASURY OF THE MYSTERIES by Nizami. English Version and Introduction by Paul Smith. New Humanity Books 2009, 11.

DIVAN OF SADI. His Mystical Love Poetry. English Version and Introduction by Paul Smith. New Humanity Books 2010.

THE SHAHNAMA OF FIRDAUSI. 8 vols. Translated by Arthur George Warner and Edmond Warner. Kegan Paul, Trench, Trubner & Co. Ltd. 1923.

FOUR EMINENT POETESSES OF IRAN by M. Ishaque. Iran Society, Calcutta. 1950 (Page 65).

OBEYD ZAKANI'S MOUSE & CAT (The Ultimate Edition) Translation & Introduction by Paul Smith New Humanity Books, Campbells Creek 2012.

PREFACE BY PRINCESS JAHAN

In the Name of God...

Thanks be to the Almighty for creating human beings with the power of speech and eloquence and grace and oration... for He is the finest of creatures having all these powers in this world.

God the All-Powerful, created the human from the earth and the other creatures who all bowed down to Him.

God gave the power of thinking to those who are wise.

God, with special power, created the human form in the best of possible shapes.

God changed the human body to the best of creatures so that he may attain perfection.

God created this complete creature to have special attributes.

Sometimes God sent prophets with miraculous powers.

Moses in the cradle was able to speak!

Sometimes God sent a prophet to reveal the happiness

of both worlds to the people.

Only God deserves to command... and those who know

His mystery.

Praise and greeting to God, Mohammed and his descendants. Mohammed is the source of religious law and during his life

the world was at its finest.

Everyone wishes for recognition in this world and to leave the world something worthwhile to be remembered by. When someone dies that one will be forgotten but if that one leaves a memory in people's minds they never forget such a one. Poems and literature are the best way to be remembered in the world.

I am... Princess Jahan, the daughter of Masud Shah and I preferred... I sometimes had to choose a lonely path. Don't choose to be alone but also don't choose to open your heart.

I composed poems all day long.

Sometimes untalented and lazy people teased

or found fault with me.

Only some people are able to compose poetry.

If composing poems is so bad we wouldn't have so many poets.

At first I thought it wasn't a good occupation because it was disapproved of and not liked in the society that I lived in.

After sometime I realized that our Prophet Mohammed's daughter composed poems and other women too, including his wife Ayesha.

I began to compose poems everyday… it became my pleasure.

If mine you will be, it is my pleasure:
and if you kill me, it is my pleasure.
You may never be mine I know but if
you remember me, it is my pleasure!

Composing poems isn't easy… you have to learn a great many things about it.

I've done my best but if there are problems with my poems, forgive me.

If I didn't do as well as I could and my poems are not as good as they should be, then please forgive me.

Please edit them yourself… help me to correct them.

Thank you.

A SELECTION OF *GHAZALS*

(The numbers are those in her *Divan*)

(1)

I can't come to see you and you can't come to see me:
a messenger better than the breeze, can there ever be?
I cannot continue this waiting for I need you so much:
O God, please show me your kindness… now, quickly!
Please come to me and rescue me for I'm so exhausted:
how much of this injustice can you keep on doing to me?
I'm so sick and tired of love… so sick and tired of love!
Come, heal my sick heart: you're my soul, undoubtedly.
What I've earned from love would amount to nothing:
in this world there's existing no faith for anyone to see.
Like a moth in a candle I continue burning in your love:
and that's not a pleasant and a bright sight, obviously.
You've no understanding of what's happening to Jahan,
without you I'm so alone: sincerity is not hidden easily.

(2)

O you source of peace and you jewel of purity too…
far away I take refuge in thoughts of coming to you.
Since you went away from me I've lay in grief's bed:
come one night, ignoring distance… loneliness undo.
When the doctor knew that I was sick he said to me:
"Meeting beloved again is the only way to cure you!"
O my love, please forgive me, but I am so afflicted…
being in this bed of separation I don't deserve to, too!
If me and what I am now feeling you are not believing,
please open your eyes, see me, and know it all is true.
The world without you… this you'd know: how I feel!
I have a face, straw-yellow… tears, blood-red through!
Isn't it enough… how much do you want me to suffer?
Who said you could be so hurtful to me, who told you?
Beloved, who is suspicious of strangers, had my heart:
attending to my wounded heart… that one did not do.
People try to not suffer too much in the world, Jahan:
a king has not to suffer inferiors, if he doesn't want to.

(5)

My beloved, why in such a vile way keep treating me:
for God's sake tell me why do you treat me so badly?
Please do not be any worse to me any more than now:
I've lost all patience grieving over you, can't you see?
Our grief is killing us... don't let it exceed its bounds:
what is the full extent of the bounds of your cruelty?
I'm in love with your long, black hair falling in braids:
this deserves, that not broken is your promise to me.
I'll go off and start painting my face with my blood,
because... my beloved, you I can't find and can't see.
If someone other than me you happen to be choosing,
I'd still not find another but you to love... obviously.
I told the breeze of your lips and your beautiful hair...
because I want that breeze to bring your smell to me.

I didn't know that caught in the net of your black hair,
I... not being able to love anyone except you, would be.
Thank God that you keep staying in the world, Jahan,
sometimes you can help any poor beggar that you see.

(6)

O my God, please have mercy on me, I'm so tired…
please allow no more injustice to me to be acquired.
I have lost all patience and I can't wait any longer:
O God, if You're kind… attention to me is required!
Be faithful to me… only one night, only one night:
do not keep my poor heart suffering, it is too tired!
You did an injustice to me and then the *kara* stone*
changed… and it gave me whatever I had requested!
My broken heart has a pain that is down so deep…
you are my only cure, heal this heart you've infested.
You are king of Jahan and the world, I am a beggar:
sometimes the beggar by a king should be noticed!
If for only one day you should be faithful to me then
all will mention your faithfulness. You interested?

* *Note: Probably a stone for reading one's fortune.*

(7)

Ah, my beloved... you, have forgotten me?
Is this a habit that you have, constantly?
I've such desire I am a compass turning on
your beauty spot: why, homeless keep me?
Be fearful of tearful sighs of broken hearts:
without a doubt prayer is effective... see?
You, you can heal me and you are my cure:
I'm sick of your love, give your cure to me!
It's so true that I'm sick of your love... but
you'd heal me... if you were kind, instantly!
You, my king, I am very worried about you;
I beg: I'd die if you asked me... immediately!
You're so cruel... ah, you have no kindness...
hard heart like a *kara* stone, is all I can see!
If I died for you it means not a thing to you:
O alchemist... nothing, is everything you see!
All the world, Jahan, to me is worth nothing
if you're being faithful to another, obviously!

(10)

A number of times I told my heart that is crazy,
that you never listen to any advice given by me.
I need to see your face, it would do me such good:
no chance... what to do with a hopeless destiny?
What to do with this heart that thinks for itself?
Truly, that one's become my life's closest enemy!
Your wine is always making my soul dead-drunk:
wise ones, don't reproach a drunken one like me!
I'm like a moth that is flying around your candle:
I want to burn my body and life away completely.
Like nightingale I cry a thousand times to see you:
your face is like a flower... I'm a thorn, all prickly!
I will cry and my tears will be a flood of kindness...
by tears, enemy's heart will be clean of rust to see.
And on the day that my body they will be burying,
I'll think of you and dust will be like heaven for me!
How can Jahan stay patient in grief of separation?
Don't burn my heart like now: it is unique, you see!

(11)

My beloved, so distant you keep me,
I don't know why:
it was so early on that you lost me...
I don't know why.
When my beloved left my sight it was no choice of mine:
that one chose to leave me suddenly...
I don't know why.
All of a sudden to me that one was paying no attention,
behaving like the world, unfaithfully...
I don't know why.
That one's secret stays hidden forever in my heart's corner:
that one told, so all knew besides me...
I don't know why.
My grief for that one is like a Mount Alvand in my heart:
you don't grieve for me hurting greatly,
I don't know why.
You didn't pay any attention to the feelings of Jahan and
you kill with eyes that fascinate me...
I don't know why.

With your charming ways you cause riots in Jahan's world:

destiny is all thorns, roses I can't see…

I don't know why.

(16)

My Sweetheart, why is it that you keep on deploring
me?
In this short life I've lived, you're never remembering
me.
I became like dust in this path of loving you like you asked,
hoping that one day from this dust... up you'd be lifting
me.
Because of the fire of your love my dust is now ash: so will
you let me be worthless... as like wind you are passing
me?
Why does your love's suffering make this fire in my heart:
as contemptible as path's dust, will you keep holding
me?
I went from friend to a stranger: did you in me lose faith?
Why estranged from yourself... are you now making
me?
You know I can't win as I am still in love with your face:
fortunately you're happy, my fortune's to be suffering
me!

My imagination went like this: if I could escape suffering,

that unfaithful sweetheart some day might be helping

me!

How could I have imagined that the healer of my sickness

sought self-health and wished this pain on unsuspecting

me?

Due to this pain in the world Jahan has tolerated from you,

I hope compassion moves you... lost, you'll not be leaving

me.

(21)

My eyes don't look at anybody except the face of my friend...
O breeze, inform that one of heart's condition... disillusioned!
Help me understand this disillusionment, my charming idol:
desperation for you broke back of my bent heart, never to mend!
That one told me to go away, or my head I'd soon be losing...
how can I leave? I've chosen beloved even if my life should end!
That one... "You chose my lips, I chose nothing but sugar!
One more time show me the sugar I want... the select blend!"
Critics keep advising me and wisely they try to prevent me:
my torn garment's soul can't accept their advice, can't pretend.
How can I not suffer... how can I not stop this grieving?
There is no choice of grief for one who bought gold, to the end!

Thieves steal caravan, from camel-driver something's taken:
how can he suffer, who on only a short-time one can depend?
"Your ruby lips are my life, give to me, soon as possible!"
Reply… "What's it profit you Jahan, your life soon will end!"
Bird of my heart out of desire will soon fly to be with you:
who'll take with bird of my heart's flight, my body to your end?

(24)

This unfaithful world, O Jahan… to not a one was ever faithful:

because of this world there's much pain, but no being merciful.

Whenever a tree wants to grow tall, full of leaves and fruit…

this world will then annihilate it… because of being wrathful!

And if the Mother-of-pearl is hidden in the endless sea of grief,

I keep wishing the noble nature's jewel isn't something fanciful.

Jewel who was like a king came from sea of kindness then went:

that none knows real worth of that one in this world, is truthful.

O God, with Your limitless kindness look upon that pearl's soul

and please keep that one in the casket of Fortune… be merciful!

I will be thankful to God... Who is the Creator of this world...
if He builds a garden of Fortune for your life, extremely thankful!
In the field of battle even the great, brave Rustom and Isfandiar*
will come again to turn your horse around... a Fortune so powerful!
No other phrase crosses my tongue but prayers for your happiness:
poor me, is in no position to help you, but to keep being prayerful.
After every inconvenience and impudence in this world Jahan did,
she will continue to pray for you with praise and eulogies, plentiful!

*Note: Two of the warrior-heroes from Firdousi's epic Shahnama.

(34)

Everyday from the depth of my heart I pray for
you!
is it really possible I could admire any more…
you?
I will instantly sacrifice all the kingdom of Persia
for your love, as I have so often said before to
you!
Although you're satisfied, all we have is suffering:
we wait for your love… whenever is good for
you!
If it satisfies you that we suffer so much… it's easy
for us to keep suffering, to keep satisfying poor
you!
My beloved, this anguished, sorrowful heart of mine
continues to miss the one it's so desperate for…
you!
If you could come over to this humble abode of mine,
that I'll do my best for you is true, for you're…
you!

Instead of my life I will sacrifice my money and gold for you but I'm ashamed for you are worth more, you!

I told that one, "Do not kill people out of selfishness: the reply, "Not worth anything is life... of poor you!"

There's no doubt that our death will be forthcoming if this heart can't be healed... that lies dying before you!

(42)

You sat yourself in my eyes, and in my heart now reside…
why is it you haven't kindly paid attention to us: why hide?
You're life to me and my afflicted body suffers separation:
sweetheart, don't keep yourself away from my body's side.
Cast a glance towards helpless ones bound by separation,
for they've no cure of release but union with you… inside.
O sweetheart, why do you continue to hide from my eyes?
In spite of my enemy's wish, your eyes towards me guide.
It is as though faithfulness has never been in this world…
it is as if kindness and faithfulness all have thrown aside.
I did nothing but have faith… so tell me what is my fault?
Why cruelly break a beached heart with oppression's tide?
And if someone made a mistake that one will make more:
O God, please us away from making more mistakes guide!
I'm poor now and I'm hated and you are the king of Jahan:
I'm in such a position I can do nothing but pray and abide.
If I can't be coming to you please tell me what I should do?
Who can take my message? Breeze, blowing far and wide?

(48)

O my heart... you should be patient in this work you do...
many, many time I have been telling you this story... true?
In the way of love and also in the desert of separation...
that you should be greatly patient is always best for you.
I've many faults... don't be asking me about my actions:
because of my actions shame fills me through and through.
And because I did not pick one flower from union's garden
a great many thorns cut into my heart and into my life too.
I happened to think that eventually I'd reach unification...
a profit from such thought was non-existent... that grew!
What was the point in you lighting a fire inside my heart?

Your bright affection has lit many a fire... isn't that true?
Due to your flashing, joyful eyes and your beautiful hair...
many was the disturbance this world that grew and grew!
Your intoxicating eyes caused Jahan to be falling into love:
there are many an injury in my heart that are caused by you.
You should be kind to me and you should be helping me...
if you don't care about me I'll stop caring for anything, too!

(50)

You are so much taller than the tallest tree
in the garden...
your face is fairer than the flowers I can see
in the garden.
You pay no attention to me... I am much smaller than you:
loving you, my heart you place permanently
in the garden.
Your face shines like the sun lighting the world and a candle
in the dark... your face is a moon for me to see
in the garden.
First thing in the morning if you listen you'll be able to hear
all the nightingales sing for you, exquisitely,
in the garden.
All the world was made fresh and new again from a breeze:
I love it... you're a flower growing fragrantly,
in the garden.
You are so much more beautiful than all those flowers
that when spring comes, open so gracefully
in the garden.

You can heal Jahan's sick heart, where can I go without you?

I remember you… from whatever I happen to see

in the garden.

(60)

My beloved, during last night I was dreaming.
A mirage or reality... I had no way of knowing.
I don't see it's the fate of in this world of Jahan
or others... for a beloved to be ever possessing.
I go crazy when I start thinking about your hair,
and your dark eyes I cannot help but... be loving.
Your mind is more important than appearance...
if not, Kai Khusrau or Afraisiyab* I'd be wanting.
With you... poison is as sweet as sugar, for me:
without you... sugar just like poison is tasting.
When I'm in the garden among all of the flowers
so fine it will be if to music of harp I'm listening.
How lovely's listening to nightingale's song and
with friends in the moonlight... wine be drinking.
This is all possible... as soon as you wish it to be!
Something better? Only conquest you're wanting?
You were drinking all in my jug quickly... so, why
am I fascinated? You never let me keep sleeping!

You were angry and could not make up your mind:

hey, don't destroy Jahan after such hard drinking!

* Note: Two kings & heroes from the Book of Kings, the Shahnama.

(73)

In this world, knowing friend or enemy isn't easy:
nothing to do but to adapt and take it easy... see?
In this world of distrust of strangers I can see that
when friends looked at me... they did not know me!
Impossible to live without your face like a candle...
like moth to candle I will burn, loving... deliberately!
Everyday my eyes are crying to you to please come:
they are full of tears: I wait your love... so patiently!
Like a nightingale everyday I'm crying for your face:
it's obvious that you will never pay attention to me.
Where can I find you? Please help me discover this,
for your love like a fire burns heart up... incessantly!
It's my fault? What's wrong with this world Jahan?
Why, why have I been placed in this way? Tell me!

(82)

My life, yes I would gladly give away

for you:

but this, is not important in any way

for you.

It seems to be your wish that I keep suffering:

but I, only wish for safety every day,

for you.

If one dies for you perhaps you'd sell yourself?

Then, I would be the first one to pay,

for you.

I'm as mad as Alexander for the Water of Life:

for I'm excited, crazy, I'd have to say:

for you.

All night you sleep soundly, but as for poor me,

awake until morning I continue to stay,

for you.

You pay me no attention in any way but I made

Jahan and the world to sit up and pay...

for you!

O my poor broken heart what could you ever do?

Not loving that one was never the way,

for you.

(97)

If that unfaithful one my true beloved is,
why continue to let me suffer... like this?
That one sleeps soundly and hates me...
dreaming my eyes are open, not like his!
I firmly believed... you were my beloved...
only a dream is such a false belief as this.
I went and I told you I'm in love with you:
you hurt me unjustly, the truth you miss!
How can I explain how much I'm hurting?
That my life is only suffering... the truth is.
When I look at all of the roses in the garden
I'd see thorns if you weren't in me, like this.
Broken heart, don't desire faith from such a
one... in the world Jahan, that one, false, is.
If that one wants me not, it's not important
for if not my beloved... he, my heartache is!

(108)

Sorrows of the world, Jahan, are upon my heart even more:
mind is more wounded by fortune's sword than ever before.
Even though the sword of fortune has wounded my heart…
there are more wounds in my heart where its secret it bore!
Why should I give any more respect to rival, assuring her?
Why should I? She's so suspicious… each time even more!
If the wolf whose fortune had no success fell into a trap…
most poor men would take the ewe… quickly out the door.
Each one in this world who has lost her life for the beloved
I will judge fairly… she's one step ahead of me… one more!
Even though inside your heart affection for me is now less,
heart's desire to reach you is more than before I can assure!
When in our cruel beloved's heart faith is not being kept…
it is strange that closer to us… is what was foreign before.

(109)

In my mind… I am always thinking about you
because I cannot come to see you, that is true.
I keep on thinking of those eyes that are yours
for those marvelous eyes lead straight to you!
I'm madly impatient to see your beautiful face:
like a baby needs milk I need you… I do… I do!
In the garden there's many a handsome cypress:
in fairness you're better… I'm being fair to you.
It's true that to die for you is always my desire:
but for you it's not important… isn't that true?
When I am seeing you I believe I'm in paradise:
all will be fine for me when I'm finally with you.
In the morning from Egypt a breeze came to me:
so anxiously I asked it if a prophet was now due.
I lost my youth and beauty because of this love:
I am old from this world… heart was broken too.
Jahan, in the world… while you continue to live,
that you'll still be in love with that one… is true!

(111)

Loving you, has broken my heart wide apart...
to explain this any more is not within my art.
I'm always being teased by those opposing me:
I suffer more than usual and grief plays its part.
My family criticizes me, opponents even more:
but they, not my family, feel sorry for my heart!
This broken heart of mine leaves that one alone:
don't imagine he is faithful, for cruelty is his art.
In Jahan is no work, except burning in this love:
every one in the world must play a grieving part.
I'm sure it would be better if I'd be like a drifter...
the world's King,* Jahan, guards a drifter's heart.

Note: The world's King is God the Almighty.

(114)

Ah my beloved, what... is wrong with you?
O why do you always treat me like you do?
You are always in a terrible mood with me:
you are always looking at me in anger too!
I burn in this love with no one beside me...
my only friend's the dirt, others are untrue!
It's true that you do not have a single friend
but good at breaking a lover's heart are you.
I can't let friends be, even if they are unkind:
in my heart this love, will be in eternity too!
If a one leaves his beloved one out of cruelty,
that's not a good and is not fair thing to do.
Jahan has loved that one for such a long time:
that I love his handsome face is true... is true!

(117)

My heart through separation sick was becoming:
my ill heart for you can't continue to be waiting.
You don't know, but being apart from your love...
my suffering defies description, tears keep falling.
O my dear sweetheart... when you are leaving me
and I'm alone... all happiness from me is leaving.
I can't wait any longer to see your handsome face:
I'm so excited to see your face I can't keep waiting.
Please be kind to a heart that is sick and suffers so:
it's a long time that this heart... you, is not seeing.
Please, O please be kind to me, because I don't feel
I'll be able to be well again separate from my darling.
Now please be kind to my grieving heart because in
Jahan and the world your face it prefers to be loving.

(120)

I am so eager to feel your long and luxurious hair...
of your eyes, beautiful and languishing... I despair.
Your hair is as dark as night, face is bright as day:
perhaps like Narcissus in water... reflecting there.
It's true that my heart has been badly burnt by you,
but, my broken heart you'd heal if only you did care.
Please, be attentive to my sick and sorry heart and
be kind, all know how I love you: beyond compare!
You're tall like the high cypress and I'm so small...
how you make this heart suffer... you are unaware.
When from your fair face your dark hair you shake,
so eager is Jahan and the world, to look and stare!

(145)

If you knew how much the world mattered... it truly

is nothing;

whatever you happen to be worried about... it really

is nothing.

In your heart should be planted faithfulness and kindness...

that I have many a humble beloved waiting on me,

is nothing.

Do not be opening my secret that is now closed to the breeze,

for that courier to betray secrets, almost breathlessly...

is nothing.

Beloved, for you that which is good and bad are the same,

you are so good that of bad your knowledge obviously

is nothing.

A beloved who is good is that one who sacrifices life for

me...

worth of any other beloved for a wise one, in any degree

is nothing.

You promised you'd not be faithful in such a way as this:

my heart, for you to worry about someone except me,

is nothing.

Do not depend on the world, Jahan, if you're not intoxicated:

if you knew world's happiness or sadness, it you'd see…

is nothing.

(146)

Fascinating beloved, patience due to your face so beautiful,
is bitter:
pain experienced from being far from you, like some hell…
is bitter.
How can I describe your pearl-like lip… that is like sugar?
The taste of the days that I am far from your face, I'll tell…
is bitter!
If hand of hope of heart was not reaching to my collar what
would I have done? Being turned from like some bad smell…
is bitter.
O philosopher, I'll not take any advice, for from what I know
I will not listen to advice about prison of idol, for that cell…
is bitter.
Kind sir, give some words that ring true then leave us alone:
you must know, any truth to one who is ignorant to tell…
is bitter.
O my dear, what should I do… for I feel like the bitter gourd?
To keep talking about one who is so sluggish, I know well…
is bitter.

O my dear, Jahan has yet to see an antidote for such a union,

have you any idea that this wine of separation is like hell...

is bitter?

(150)

Someone who is in love with me took my hand last night,
but I said, "Please forget me, dismiss me from your sight!"
That one: "What's wrong, is it because I took your hand?"
I answered, "The one I'm in love with is not here tonight."
I continued, "I swear that as long as I live I'll love that one:
if that one destroys my life, I will say it's that one's right!"
Then I whispered, "I swear that I'll never, I'll never give up,
I will never give up… until that one's kind to me one night!"
I was asked: "You *sure* you want to be faithful to that one?"
I said, "I'll be faithful, until I'm *always* in that one's sight!"
Please come, heal sick heart's longing, for from loving you,
for me to attempt doing anything, is now a terrible plight!
For you I'm ready to immediately sacrifice my life if asked:
you don't show kindness of demanding that right outright!
Certainly, the cypress is a tree that is tall and it is strong,
but don't forget the other trees taller than its great height!
Only one thing that I know and it's… I'm in love with you:
I've lost my heart… you steal it from me as if it's your right.
On the chessboard of life it seems your king has failed me…
and a mere pawn such as I am can never overcome a knight.

Nightingales can't sit in your fair face as in the rosebushes;

but in this world, Jahan, many are the nightingales in sight.

(155)

I have become so used to being in love with you:
that all this world of Jahan worships you, is true.
Because of loving you, my eyes continue to weep:
there is not a doubt that deep inside I suffer too.
My tired soul is like a parrot that having tasted
your sweet lip... only remembers being with you.
Your face is so beautiful, so attractive that I was
silent, but seeing you I talk of you... all day too!
You're so handsome and you're also so tall... but,
because of loving you my body is frail... it is true!
You keep playing with me like it's a game of polo:
I'm your ball... you hit me anywhere you want to.
Each day I keep pressing up against myself and if
Jahan's into this habit, it's because of loving you.

(163)

Today is such a special day, the like of which no one has ever seen,

from breeze comes scent like of which no one smelling has been.

In the morning, ear of my heart heard voice of the invisible speaker,

saying this day is joyful… especially for son of the king and queen.

It may be autumn at the moment but great God with His kindness

in the garden of happiness is quite able to turn everything to green.

The flowers of happiness always grow from the rosebush of hope…

otherwise, no one is ever able to pick such a flower in this season.

All of the people are searching… the sky for crescent of this night

and upon this special night the sun shining brightly has now risen.

During this night of fasting we've much happiness and great joy,
because we all have as special guest the son of the king to be seen.

The gazelle of Tartary has a bag of musk that comes from China,
that never inhaled the generosity and the kindness of your garden.

When in the garden the cypress saw your stature that is so high…
its back it bent because it shy and humble before you had been.

Ever since the attention that you are giving to all was lost to me…
I've suffered so much and tears as streams of blood can be seen.

I, Jahan… pray and am willing to pay due admiration to the world,
but, let me ask this, "Why, from God… so far away have I been?"

(198)

Loving your beautiful face isn't some new thing

for me:

like an old friend is to be in your love, burning,

for me.

It is such a long time that I have been burning in your

love and it's nothing new, this... you to be loving,

for me.

Colour and a beautiful face is nothing new for flowers:

it's an old garden if at the world one is looking,

for me.

Many are the problems one has if one is falling in love:

such a long time for love to try to be avoiding...

for me.

It is such a long time, a long time... I've been loving you:

your beautiful face to keep loving is no new thing

for me.

Don't you be asking Jahan to begin a love that is new:

it is such a long time for a heart, to keep losing...

for me.

(200)

Don't ask my heart… in Jahan or the world, it's homeless:
it's worried all the time about love and it's lost… hopeless!
After I saw that one… tall and handsome like the spruce…
every single day I was suffering and crying, I was helpless!
I cannot compare that one to a cypress… that one's so tall!
Comparing that one, (my heart and soul), is totally useless!
I cannot compare that one to a cypress, that one is so tall…
comparing that one, O my heart and soul… is… pointless!
I fell deep into love… into that dark eye, that thick eyebrow:
but why you will never, ever notice me, I can never… guess!
O yes, it's true I have even compared you to the bright sun:
why do you keep hiding your fair face from me nevertheless?
I have lost all of my patience and sighs are leaving my heart:
I worry about my fate… I will die or live? Ah… such stress!
It would be better if my heart should be avoiding that one…
because, that one wants my heart in that one's trap, no less!
O please, help me… you are so kind and I am so very tired…
all this is cried by your lovers' everyday… ah, what a mess!

Broken heart, the reliable Almighty helps you gain control…

time's gone, Jahan and the world one day death will caress!

(201)

Your life bestowing kindness hope of the sinner
is...
anyone who doesn't believe this, that one a sinner
is.
O you who're a sinner who's so sinful don't deny it:
rely on God's kindness, for it right for him and her
is.
One shouldn't be disappointed by the Friend's help,
even though in minds of many people... this error
is.
I thank God, for even with such sins as I have done
He still raining His mercy on me, a great sinner,
is.
Although I have grief of loving that one in my heart,
everyone, that such sorrow's inside me, a knower
is.
Night and day, separation and union are not apart...
O my Friend, you should know that nothing truer
is.

If I'm such a sinner, I'll be relying on such kindness,

because I know Beloved always the kind forgiver

is.

If my Beloved asks about me, a lifeless one in love...

say this quickly: this one, due to wish of another,

is.

Your drunken eye stole Jahan's heart, and her life...

You oppressor, your actions like some other lover

is.

(209)

During autumn look at the roses... how beautiful they are;
it seems the grass is a workshop of dyers from near and far.
And it seems the autumn breeze all of this colour brought:
it did not bring the roses... it just brought the roses colour.
It's because of that One, your ruby lip's as sweet as sugar:
it is only because of that One, that you merciful to me are.
The Painter of this world created the colour for this garden
unless you believe it's autumn breeze or something similar.
Although Jahan deserves no thoughts of castles built in air,
she cannot help thinking and feeling about you... from afar.

(230)

Between Jahan, the world and all in it... is separation:
I am not in fear of my enemy or friend's consternation.
If I'm like a word in the peoples' mouth it isn't strange
because inside the shell is always the pearl's location.
To one who leaves the world with its good and bad...
the people's praises or slander causes no perturbation.
"If you are simple and pure you will be seeing the Sun:
if the dark night is before you... have no trepidation."
I've placed this couplet by Hafiz in my poem because
this *ghazal* of his I love deeply... without reservation.
O my friend, I have no complaints about my enemies:
I only complain of friends... with enemy's disposition.
My temperament's garden's breeze is jealous, impure:
I hear it has ambergris scent from a heavenly station.
It could be likened to a bud the breeze easily blows...
and after being blown it's feeling joyful exhilaration.
Jahan, the world's beautiful but don't leave the grass:
place for enlightened ones waits near river's location.

(281)

O my heart, the world isn't faithful so I've no remedy:
in this world except blood and grief, nothing I can see.
Try to take care and not worry about the world, Jahan,
for who is really ruling the world is unclear, obviously.
So you try hard to be happy and also not to be worried
for the world except for this has nothing for you or me.
I've lost all of my patience from grieving in this world…
heart not weakened by world's grief's an impossibility.
One died, one lost heart from world's ups and downs…
good reason for one to stay here could be called 'irony!'
All in love with you are moon-faced, cypress statured…
unlike those I'm not tall like a cypress… can't you see?
If you happen to come over to this sad house of mine…
for you I would quickly be sacrificing anything, even me.
I have been weeping so much for you my beloved that in
these eyes there's not one tear left… it's true! Look, see!
Because of this long separation all my patience has gone:
again I ask… "Why can't Jahan be with you? Tell me!"

(311)

O God, there is no end to Your kindness and grace:
to praise You truly, my mouth is not the right place.
That one who's been trusting upon the Sea of Truth
is a sheep with no need again of the shepherd's face.
Of that treasure of pearl of the word You gave me,
I have no interest in security for it, not even a trace.
Leaf of tree not praising or whispering Your name...
such a one in the garden obviously hasn't any place.
Flower that has not been opened by Your kindness,
I'm sure that such a one takes up no garden's space.
Why ask about such impure feelings of a weakling?
No one pays attention... sees them as no disgrace.
That One is like a cypress growing in heart's dust...
in the garden not a one is as tall, or has such grace.
Except for Court of Your kindness, world Creator,
you know only too well I've no place to go, no place.
During this being far from my beloved in the world,
that I have no protection but your Court, is the case.
You have many a slave in the world, including Jahan;
but like Jahan, none as lonely out of all the populace.

(348)

Is it only some wind or is it really a breeze from paradise?
Beloved, but for your angelic nature… paradise is only lies.
Sound of nightingale and harp and sound of the *tar* is good
and it's so good that through field, river… water supplies.
I should always be able to see your face that is like heaven:
you've the right to show whatever face to me that applies.
Although I may not know everything there is one thing I do,
if those repulsive ones embrace you nothing good in this lies.
I could never leave this love of you… listen: in the beginning
God creates me… this love of you, me completely occupies.
In the past I didn't give thanks for my destiny… I know this
is the reason why my fortune every kind of good luck defies.
I can't say that your love for my bones is a worthless thing,
for Jahan's ashes will make bricks for the world's supplies!

(429)

Look at the world's garden, what will it bring forth again?
Of the people, whose fortune will it use again, and when?
Who'll once again drink the cup of the night of the world?
Who'll wake up sad and poor because of the world, again?
Who will be falling into the trap… that's set by the world?
Whose hand will it be… that is drawn by the world's pen?
Whose ear will be hearing the song of the chrysanthemum?
Whose heart will it be to be made to moan there and then?
How many of our dearest friends it wants to bury in dust?
How much does it care about the poor people… and when?
Whose garden with any hope left will be bearing the tulip?
Whose garden of fortune will be a bearer of thorns, again?
Whose kingdom's bed this time is falling in the deep well?
Whose fortune's star by the world, Jahan, is melted again?

(517)

Breeze gave me the message that the beloved
is coming:
that one, to heal the pain of being separated,
is coming.
Over the field breeze brought a message to the grass that
the sweet-smelling rose into the garden's bed
is coming.
O my heart, although you are far away from the beloved,
thank God for end of night of being separated
is coming.
Though you're sorrowful from being far from your beloved,
don't worry, you will be happy when beloved
is coming.
If I'm far from your beautiful face this New Year's Day,
then for you... this weak body being sacrificed
is coming.
City of Saba has reminded the hoopoe that is auspicious
that love's nightingale... back to garden's bed
is coming.

The bright, shining sun gives a sign of that one's coming:

again invisible world's voice into Jahan's head

is coming.

(598)

I heard this message brought by breeze in the morning:
"Poor heart of mine, the rose has blossomed, be waking!"
Ground's covered with tulips, lilies, gillyflower, box-trees:
the ground with the songs of nightingales is clamouring.
The breeze brought the wine-cup and the rose has bloomed:
from over the field we could hear sounds of wine drinking.
And now I sit down on the grass in this beautiful garden…
and some sounds from the invisible world now I'm hearing.
Beloved's face is like a rose and lip is like the wine-cup's lip:
and it is because of this that my mouth the wine is tasting.
My heart had become lost to me because of separation…
now my heart is alive for your sweet breath I'm smelling.
Store in the bazaar selling perfumes had to shut its doors
for your lips like pearls came and forced its quick closing.
When the nightingale listened to all of the crying of Jahan
that nightingale was agitated then silent it was becoming.

(600)

O yes, how to make love, my heart
knows well,
your lip to lover, a kiss to impart...
knows well.
When the heart is in love then that life is alive!
This game of love and life my heart
knows well.
My heart has been fired by clay of separation:
how to be burnt up? It... this art
knows well.
In a dream of you, you invite my eyes to come:
a dream, to play hospitality's part,
knows well.
The love that I have for your face is a real love,
but it's a false kindness your heart
knows well.
You are Mahmud* and I am in love with you...
to be like Ayaz, your heart its part
knows well.

My heart keeps on beating like that of a pigeon,

for to play me like a king, your heart

knows well.

Yes, this heart of mine is still in love with you:

for to love… Jahan's heart, this art

knows well.

* Note: Mahmud was a king whose slave Ayaz he loved as the Beloved.

(603)

The oppression of this world, Jahan, is so overwhelming…
around everyone's heart it wants a chain to be tightening.
It is true that because of what the world's accomplished,
the tree of hopefulness withered… ceased to be existing.
It is also true that from the garden of the heart of Jahan,
each leaf eventually into a corner that one was scattering.
The meadow's cypress of the wishes of these lives, away
by the hand of that one's oppression was sent… blowing.
I'm crying because of what the world is doing once again!
How very much that one, us to keep suffering is wanting!
What to do with my heart? Because of my dearest friend
that one takes no advice, of heart's grief's never thinking.
It is time to say that this world, Jahan, has placed some
cotton of neglectfulness in ear that that one is forgetting.

(611)

Nobody can knock at door that is not opened by anybody:
that one is not a real man who to others doesn't act justly.
That man who is wise does not rely upon the world, Jahan:
only be kind… to death no one takes anything, obviously.
Those who were good… kind to others in the world, Jahan,
didn't lose anything… they live, they gained immortality!
A person who gained wealth through property of another,
ah, brother… that anybody cared for that one, did you see?
If you've mines full of treasure and the empire of Solomon
then about what you'll take when you die, think seriously!
But, if you are able to help any of the people who are poor,
don't stop yourself doing this for it's admirable, you see?
So open wide the door of kindness and generosity because
opening of Heaven's door to you is then a real possibility.

(646)

Nearly everyone in the world seeks power and money:
not believing in God they cause suffering constantly.
Jahan, a world this is full of evil and ignorance, with
such dangerous, faithless people, to avoid... obviously.
They have only fear of each other and why is this so?
They flee away from each other like gazelle does flee!
If somebody gets something that one will hide it and if
somebody else finds it, fight to the death you will see!
The world is not eternal, it has a beginning and an end:
yet in the world, Jahan, people are very rarely friendly.
All they want is your power and money, nothing else...
staying with you, only if you've money and are happy.
My heart is like a gazelle that stays in the mountain...
it has become lost and I can't find it for the sake of me!

(686)

Many flowers can be grown with soil and water,
and eventually beloved will be submissive to her.
In garden of the heart at morning, all the flowers
the breeze will blow towards nightingale's bower.
Every time that one's beautiful eyes look my way
my heart loses patience, due to eyebrow's power.
Chinese portrait painter your hair cannot portray:
your beautiful face smells good…O such fine hair!
And if the good bride wishes to witness your soul,
if she weds him tell groom to bare his soul to her.
O son, please keep far away from envy and greed,
because that's a tree bringing nothing but rancor.

(707)

God will solve this problem for me,
one day:
God will open the door successfully,
one day.
O my poor heart, suffer no more... for through
Him my problem will go, eventually,
one day.
You shouldn't be appealing to people to help:
He helps, opening door of prosperity
one day.
I've lost patience, having no help except His:
perhaps God's grace will heal me...
one day.
O God, please open blessing's door for me...
if You don't, who will... eventually,
one day?
My poor heart, during this night of separation
wait until door's opened completely,
one day.

Ah Jahan... your foot is tied down with grief:
prayer will open door for you and me
one day.

(725)

O my friends, my friends… please, please… help me:
please be sympathetic, as I have fallen in grief's sea.
Does anyone treat a friend with cruelty such as this?
Why act like a stranger? Be faithful to us, please be!
I'm a lonely, sad person… in grief's sea I'm drowned:
O unjust friend, for just once be sympathetic to me!
I will cry, "O my God!" for you, for He told us that
one should avoid being believer in friends, suddenly.
From the cruelty of the people my heart is sorrowful:
but, I will try to travel without burdens in sin's sea.
O Jahan! Such a dark fortune! O life! A darker face!
How much do you want to offend people's sensitivity?
O tears, O heartache… to me how much more pain?
If you torment the people, Jahan will be killed by me!

(746)

O my wounded, separated heart, your life is so distressed:

you're always in the bright fire like the hair of the Beloved.

I'm the one who is lost but every day I find You get better;

this is all I keep doing when from Your face I'm distanced.

Though You've no knowledge of my deplorable condition,

my eyes watch for You... every day and night I'm focused.

You told me, "Try to be patient and do not suffer anymore:

happiness comes through sorrow, and thorn rose caused."

We are Your path's dust and You are a beautiful cypress:

it is not a difficult thing if one day You by us have passed.

In the garden the drunken narcissus has raised his head...

when can I say that Your charming eye, him has defeated?

Though You've many lovers in the world, including Jahan,

it is nothing if You kindly pay just one attention, Beloved.

(751)

A heart that is wounded is in love with the Beloved's hair,
that one couldn't be patient… patience left then and there.
O my Idol, You've stolen my heart and now want my life,
although I've no way out of such grief from love's despair.
My eyes that know not sleep are dependant on this love…
heart, how often I have warned you about a faithless affair.
Although you bring shame upon me, O my Idol, my Ideal,
I am still proud of this love bringing such sorrow, I swear!
The ball… my heart, has become tired of Your polo game:
because there's no winner like in the game of love I declare.
What's my jasmine-smelling cypress done with my heart?
You took my heart and gave it to plane tree without a care!
I had a fresh heart… as fresh as the face of my loved One:
see how grief of world and Jahan fades it… too much wear!
When will You and poor old me be coming together again?
What's my fortune? Who'll be the lucky one? Please share!
Those pious people make some effort in this world… Jahan,
for what is left here by kings is only a memory to compare.

(759)

I told myself if You return some attention I may be paid...
You returned, I was more distressed from Your loving aid.
O God, who will tell such a King about how I am feeling?
Will this One ever remember me... a mere dervish maid?
You went far away... I couldn't sleep from pain and grief:
my eyes on path, ears to door, perhaps news from an aide?
O breeze, tell to that One... "Through grief of separation,
how long is a person to suffer searching for You, waylaid?"
You should be kind to me, because I am in deep trouble...
if God's made you wealthy, to your poor subjects give aid!
I have been put in a predicament hoping for Your kindness.
I wouldn't be in trouble if I had not been in love I'm afraid.
O hard heart, how long am I to be kept sad and ashamed?
Such sorrow will make me turn upside down, to be flayed.
Soon as I promise You, I've then broken all other promises:
when sorrowful with You, happiness is no longer my trade.
Your bow did attack my heart with thousands of arrows...
I've given my heart for You... but life of Jahan is my blade.

(768)

O my heart, you are full of grief and you hope to be healed: don't despair:

the day when you'll be with Beloved will soon be revealed: don't despair.

O my heart, you are so distressed, separated from your Beloved:

in the world be bewildered, but from hope of being settled don't despair.

O my eyes, if you're not patient when you want to see Beloved,

if all the time you're staring at the arrow's sharpened head, don't despair.

And if you do not know a single thing about the world's mystery,

eventually all the sorrow of the world will pass... be dead: don't despair.

O nightingale, don't let separation from rose silence you a moment:

rejoice in the garden so that to the Gardener can be said... "Don't despair!"

You who made me to be far from Your rosy cheeks, You will be
separation's thorn's salve one day: I'll say to You instead,
"Don't despair!"
O my heart, if you are the slave of separation's thorn don't be afraid,
all of a sudden the rose will be coming in the garden's bed: don't despair.
Behind the curtain of the sorrow of separation stands a kind bride:
man cannot hide forever from such a one and never be wed: don't despair.
In the end the morning of union will defeat the night of separation:
from east the shining sun will rise so let it again be said…
"Don't despair!"
How long do you want to search the world, Jahan… like Alexander?*
Be like Khizer*… drink of the water of eternal life instead!
Don't despair!

---

*Note: Alexander searched in the Land of Darkness with Khizer as his guide seeking the Water of Life (Immortality). Only Khizer found it as he was pure.

(769)

O my bewildered heart, from this world's sorrow,

do not grieve:

world's condition goes up today, down tomorrow,

do not grieve.

If this world's hurricane threw you into blazing fire of love,

if your honour is upon the ground or even below:

do not grieve.

And if you happen to live life like Jacob in the house of grief,

that lost Joseph will return again to Canaan, so

do not grieve.

Every day seek and don't be hopeless about God's kindness,

people who have hope find what they hope for, O

do not grieve!

If your aim is for the Kaaba don't turn off from desert's path,

depend on this suffering, in thorn-bush don't go.

Do not grieve!

Pain from that One's better than healing: sit... be patient!

If you cannot find a way to heal heart's sorrow,

do not grieve.

For in the world there's no trust, so might as well be happy:

water comes back to the dried-up river… and so

do not grieve.

Gardener, best wait, be patient with this trouble with crows:

nightingale will return with a frenzied oratorio…

do not grieve.

Jahan, how long you want heart to suffer due to this world?

Your life settles down, if not today, tomorrow.

Do not grieve!

(777)

My heart had given up its life through separation from you
again,
but my soul cried from happiness because of reaching you
again.
Suddenly the world was given the joyful news of your return,
my sad soul came back to life when you didn't say adieu
again.
Heart was desiring to know of the condition of the beloved:
it let me see it leaving, but hid when it returned… anew
again.
I asked heart, "Why did you leave me? Please tell me now!"
The reply… "Silence! My love and soul back to you flew
again!"
We should be giving the joyful news to the river and meadow
that the beautiful cypress such a sudden return did do
again.
We gave away our lives when we saw with all of our eyes…
that charming garden's cypress came back to me and you
again.

Thanks be to God, that the peacock of my so sorrowful heart
returned from soul's garden when showing beauty on cue,
again.

Heart saw that one's pearly lip, mused this with admiration:
"Look at my soul's pearl, beloved's mine it's gone back into
again."

You told me one day you will return because of my sorrow!
"You of the sorrowful face, with you will I ever be through
again?"

That one who you made happy, being happy being with you,
was in a hidden corner, but finally did come back to you
again!

O Jahan, though you became old through days of separation:
my eyes watched you, I worry about you, narcissus you…
again!

Soul's nightingale became silent from thorn of separation:
but on seeing your rosy face, my song came loud and true
again!

(789)

It is a crying shame that this world helps those who are mean:
one needs many compassionate people to change what has been.
This old world of ours is full of iron and copper and also tin:
even gold and silver will be melted down by its great oppression.
Golden light of humanity with its oil will always be burnt:
see such unfaithfulness, candle burns with fire that is unseen!
The selfish keep birds and partridges at home and feed them:
hunting in hills, deserts, fields... they return with bait: so mean!
Because of unfaithfulness of this cruel, this oppressive world,
the bird of my heart that can fly in the sky will never be seen.
To whom can I tell the story of this world... that is so cruel?
Only the breeze, for my confidant the breeze has always been.

Please, be passing on this message from Jahan to the world: do not be proud anymore that it is… a pride, that is so obscene!

(785)

You are like Mahmud, I am like his slave Ayaz... praising You.
You need no one and all the world's people need You... is true!
Breeze, how long do you want to play with hair of Beloved?
I'm burning with jealousy: leave game you play, our Friend too!
All who looked at those archways to pray to, Your eyebrows, are unbelievers if they don't pray at your arches of prayer, to You!
I am the one who is poorest slave among all of Your slaves: with Your protection of poor me, be kind to me please... do!
Quicksilver tears on my golden face I'll certainly be coining: when body is melting in fire of generosity of spendthrift You!
When cypress sees Your tall form it will from jealousy make a row... just walk gracefully until that cypress is finished... through!

Sometimes it is best You avoid giving what I need, Beloved, soul dies bearing Your airs… don't be putting on airs, will You?

Though soul despises unfaithful, unfavourable world again; that small, weak sparrow can't stand before falcon's grip, is true!

As long as world exists Jahan, from necessity it is like this: for every up there is a down, for every down there is an up… too!

(801)

It is not worth asking for even one favour from anybody…
You alone in this world give daily bread to anyone like me.
When I came into the world I realized no one is oneself…
it is only the kindness of Yours that rescued us, obviously!
No one finds the right way if one asks an unworthy one…
separate the Friend's way, from that of anyone unworthy.
In all this world there is not one anything similar to You:
come to our rescue with Your grace… and please help me!
In this boundless sea of Yours I am such a small thorn…
and a small thorn can never be found upon top of the sea.

(814)

O God, please give my afflicted heart some good news...
and do something so those I love... me again will choose.
Take notice of my spiritual views and also of my religion,
victory to my enemies, strangers, friends: nothing to lose!
Heal me with happiness because I am tired of suffering...
make one worthless worthy with Your grace: me peruse!
We cannot find our way without a leader who is wise...
those following be impressed that to follow You I choose.
Shed light, show pleasantly candle of the deceased's face:
to heart's melancholic bird give plumage that will enthuse.
When arrows of an evil event are shot by Fortune's bow...
give my heart and my soul a shield... so that I cannot lose!
On Resurrection Day You forgive sins because of prayers:
forgive all of my sins from my cries at dawn, if You choose.

(844)

About my life my mind feels no tranquility:
I am constantly surprised about my destiny.
I've seen oppression cause exile, it's familiar:
see how I'm feeling about its close proximity!
I returned from beloved and I am bewildered...
to break up with this lover was to punish me?
Although the world with poor me has fought...
of my God I'll not stay hopeless, God help me!
If around that one's body I can't place my hands,
my hands will weep tears of blood... continually.
Your ruby lips are water of life for thirsty ones...
water from your lustrous lips give, immediately!
I'm as my enemy wished: that unfaithful beloved
never mentions this loving friend, it's a tragedy!
I continue to sit at door of Union with that one,
hoping my sweetheart will show me some mercy.
They ask, "Jahan, from world, you've got what?"
All I have is regret for all I have done, obviously.

(849)

In separation's dark night I'm wretched and burning, like a candle:
that One laughs like a flower while I burn, weeping like a candle.
My heart is burning up and the smoke is rising into the blue...
from fire of grief for that One, my life is spluttering like a candle.
Tell this to that beautiful sun, "Rise from the east's hopeful horizon
like a dawn... before Your face life I'll be sacrificing like a candle!"
There's nothing beside me in bed except grief of longing for that One:
every night until morning, me... sorrow keeps melting, like a candle.
My One who burns the world's candle sits happy at some party
with a heart without any worries, while I'm spluttering like a candle.

Into the depth of my soul that One previously spun such deep longing

that each night and morning my whole body is burning like a candle.

As long as the fire of grief's longing for that One is in Jahan's soul

I'll stay distressed, wounded, confused and muttering… like a candle.

(862)

I eat my heart out in this world from grief due to separation:
I have lost all of my patience, now I have only consternation.
You keep saying, "Be patient!" Go, tell separation how long
I should be patient, for I taste only bitterness of separation.
Is it possible You've not experienced separation's intensity?
Let not one night of separation be any person's destination.
We are intoxicated by Your flirtatious, wild, narcissus eyes:
I am sorry because of Your eyebrows arched for elimination!
Should I fight the world… or separation caused by Beloved?
These are two problems that're difficult to find any solution.
You must know in this world nothing happens of any worth,
so let no one in it be not with it, unless as a real companion.
This world Jahan, is so unfaithful I've lost patience with it;
how long will I suffer… hateful, bombastic communication.
If wealth could come my way and world became my friend,
with six arched-porches I'd build a hut, permanent location.

(863)

My back became arched over from the sorrow

of love;

foot of my heart's wounded by thorn, the arrow

of love.

No one can ever be mentioning the name of my heart…

in bazaar I sell life for what I beg, buy or borrow

of love.

This sorrow and patience love demands is a heavy price:

O God, from this heart please lift off the sorrow

of love.

O my poor heart, try to be compatible with separation…

like this will be condition, today and tomorrow,

of love.

O fellow Muslims, each time it starts again in my heart,

this grief from separation, hurts into the marrow

of love.

Separation from Beloved built a house of patience for me

called 'Success with Unity': an architect I know

of love.

My face changed and finally became yellow like straw...

in this world, Jahan, it is merely a relic, on show,

of love.

(865)

Help me... my heart makes me wander, searching
for love:
I don't know how long it will be slavishly obeying
for love.
My pain will heal? I am afflicted by the day of separation:
except union with you, this world holds no healing
for love.
All are confused as to what one's work in life should be...
I'm one in the world's kingdom... homeless, looking
for love.
If I can be with that one on feast of a New Year's Day...
my life bringing grief be sole under your foot lying...
for love.
One night come and become one of the army of Dervishes:
one flag will be raised for you: love's king... flying,
for love.
In the sky no moon will ever shine that is like your face...
as tall as you no cypress will in garden be growing,
for love.

Like the Huma* cast a lucky shadow on our home one night,

then by sun of your face the palace will be glowing

for love.

Arrow of your eyelashes quiver from bow of your eyebrow

struck my heart! How to get it out as it is slaying

for love?

If you hit with polo-stick I'll fall your on foot like polo ball:

I'll never bow and in defeat this field be leaving...

for love!

If that one uses sword, those hands I will kiss like a rein...

same, if that one pulls hands then my lap is hurting,

for love.

*Note: Huma... a bird like the phoenix that symbolizes the Beyond State of God.

(872)

I've promised not to fall in love with a phantom, one I don't see:
with such an impossible relationship... all patience has left me.
My dream of you, my dream lover, closed for me the way of sleep
for my body was wearing your dream, like a dream so dreamily!
For you I abandoned head, life, my religion and also my heart:
won't you please tell me... who forgave my blood for you, tell me.
Please, on bereaved and bewildered me have some mercy, please:
because... this weariness of mine is as perfect as it could ever be!
I am swearing this by the beautiful gazelle-like eyes of that one:

by that one's exquisite moon-like face, crescent eyebrows to see;

and by that one's face like a rose and that one's jasmine cheeks,

by that hair perfumed with ambergris, lips drip water of purity;

and by those thirsting, loving lips joining mine in my dreaming,

and that one's tall, graceful walk and stature like a young tree...

that during the night of separation from that one's moonlike face

Jahan's weariness from being without you is beyond me, sincerely!

That one, "You are a frenzied nightingale in love with rose's face:

O go away, you poor lover, don't be complaining anymore to me!"

(892)

What should I do beloved, who should I tell my heart's grief to?
From loving you I've gained nothing except grief, isn't that true?
O breeze, please inform my beloved of the condition of my heart,
that Jahan is now feeling so foolish from grieving because of you.
You know that I don't take a moment's notice of you in my mind:
be careful, that taking notice of heart hurting... you do not do!
If a chicken should want grain it will surely be caught in a net,
in other words... one who is wise isn't caught in grief's net is true.
Most of mankind have as their great desire all of the *huris* of Paradise...

but what should I do for my mind desires to have nothing but you!

I still remained faithful to my hope that we would experience union.

Ah… such a thought was mistaken, I imagined something untrue!

Jahan will take the regret from this love to the Resurrection Day…

that she'll never be honoured by reaching union with you is true!

(908)

With your face I could have lost faith's backgammon...
for I have thrown the marble dice to gain your affection.
My soul's sorrow separate from you isn't just of today,
such sorrow loving you causes... goes on and on and on.
Like a bewildered moth, circling candle of friend's face...
this world, and that one later on, for me have now gone.
My heart and soul and youth became a stranger to me,
when I became like a dog in your alley hoping for a bone.
For years during the ups and downs of separation's days
the wind of the last faith in the world, Jahan has blown.
I became passionate... mad about you, so eager for you:
I often look through my eyes, you they've never known.
My tongue was like an eloquent parrot in admiring you:
from grief of separation, now worse than a dove I moan.
Although I will blame my rival, like a cypress I still rise
even though with you I haven't yet any night of union.
My soul, so long since Jahan saw you come in the door:
because of grief from separation... like wax I melt down.

(1117)

You are my Layla* and my sick heart you can heal:
I'm Majnun and there's no home where home I feel.
You're Shirin… you are waiting for Khosrau Parviz:
I'm Farhad and I've lost you, my Shirin… my ideal!
You're Shirin and you are my heart, you're my heart!
I'm Khosrau and far away from you all seems unreal.
You're Ozra and I'm in love with you, with only you:
I'm Vamegh… this sick heart of mine, O please heal!
You're Golshe and you keep reminding me of a rose!
I'm Varge… I'm so far away from you, can't you feel?
You're my beautiful Wis and you've stolen my heart:
I'm Ramin, loving you I'm burning like fanatic's zeal.
I admire God because the Almighty's Eternal and He
gave me a soul and faith and God is kind and Real!

*Note: All the names in this poem are of famous lovers in Persian Literature.

(1145)

It's very pleasing for you to pick a rose in the morning,
and also in the morning… beloved's lips to be kissing;
and to take the beloved's hand and walk in the garden,
and into your beloved face to be looking is so pleasing.
Walking beside river where willow and plane-tree grow
hearing the nightingale's song, a cup of wine drinking.
Up into the face of your tall beloved you can gaze and
to that nightingale's song you'll never tire of listening.
Every day I can go and look at the meadow and cypress
and there's for me nothing but a deep nostalgia coming.
Heart of mine, you're broken because you love the world:
I couldn't a thing better than Jahan in a world be finding.
There wasn't a thing I wanted that I was able to obtain:
but every day you're getting better and yourself creating.

(1146)

The breeze of New Year's here, let us a celebration
take:
the hand of your beloved... quickly into the garden
take.
In the garden I can smell the violet and the wallflower,
crying in the garden, nightingale to intoxication...
take.
O gardener... listen to the singing of the nightingale and
make the rose happy and the thorns to incineration
take.
My beloved will come even though competitor is jealous:
minstrel come... earn your pay, them to competition
take.
O breeze, when in the gardens please tell to my beloved,
"You are all that I desire... come, you to unification
take."
I'm joyful for my beloved comes... so tell my rival, "Leave!"
I will talk of beloved, or me like Mansur* for execution
take.

*Note. See note to the following ghazal.

(1161)

Please come and heal this broken heart of mine,

I'm sad away from you, come… make me shine!

If you were me you'd understand how I'm feeling:

be like the narcissus and make your eyes supine.

Don't you listen to those people with big mouths,

just try to care for your beloved, beloved of mine!

I don't hide my pure love from eyes of the people…

Lord, clean that one's mind of memories not fine.

My heart is broken like petals of the fallen tulip:

like a burnt-yellow rose is this sad heart of mine.

My dearest beloved, those wagging tongues told

you to stay away from your lover who's in decline.

Even if they want to execute you do not complain…

your thoughts and your actions to Mansur* incline.

*Note: Mansur is Mansur Hallaj (Died 919 A.D.), the famous and infamous Perfect Master who was executed for declaring his Godhood with the words Anal Haq, "I am the Truth!" For his poems see my 'Mansur Hallaj: Selected Poems' New Humanity Books, 2012.

(1176)

O form, tall like the shy cypress, with a face like the jasmine...
your lovers who desire you, O soul, are longing for the garden.
Until that rose has become scattered from shyness of your face,
the drooping cypress out of shame is continuing to never listen.
If in garden you are breathing for a moment towards the stream,
from your shy form's stature the elm tree is shivering once again.
And if the narcissus is seeing your eye, who will be lifting its head?
If you open your mouth, the bud will stay closed, there and then.
If the violet sees your curl, black as night... it's strange that from
being polite it's not kissing your feet's dust, as I am again, again.

If the tulip has one look at your complexion it would not bloom...
and from the shame of comparison lying scattered is the jasmine.
If you keep combining loving glances with your curl and your mole
without a doubt... O soul, to Zanzibar's army chaos will happen!
And even those blind eyes of Jacob will become full of certainty...
when the breeze is carrying news of the garment... there and then.
Without your face... the world is not seen by these eyes of Jahan:
you, quickly come again, our bright eyes are crowd's candle... when.
If messenger from Egypt comes to Canaan without bringing news,
becoming the house of grief because of that... is Paradise's garden.

Have some mercy on us lovers and let your drunken eyes speak,

in Jahan's world, quarrel how long makes blood flow and it darken?

(1234)

The clouds are trying to hide the moonlight…
many people I asked to help me in my plight.
You pay no attention to me, what should I do?
Separated, heart burns… a harvest it will ignite.
Being far from beloved isn't easy: such a storm
rages in my heart I'll need Noah's ark in sight!
I'm on fire but my beloved would melt any iron…
I flog a dead horse with this burnt heart tonight!
I thought all my sighs might make an impression
but… you beloved, have burnt me away, outright.
On New Year's Day in garden, message of breeze
is the rose's suicide the nightingale's cry will incite.
Jahan, in the world what is the nightingale's song?
Rose's pride is in a beautiful face that does delight.

(1237)

O beloved, the scent of your hair to the wind... for my sake,
don't give:
news of my tired honour and promise to others don't take...
don't give.
Heart, listen to a little advice from this one with no power...
to give yourself to any heavenly rivals is a mistake:
don't give!
Although it wasn't your choice to be a man or a woman...
the reins of your good intentions for teachers to take,
don't give.
Although today there is desire for the face of the beloved...
hope of my union's promise to morning to forsake...
don't give.
To your soul whom separation's pride causes water on face:
in... to the slanderous gossip those evil enemies make,
don't give.
Heart, drive off from this day any hope of union with idols:
a talk to me of the beloved's past ways is a mistake...
don't give.

To Jahan, how much cruelty, lack of kindness will you show?
Talking with you is cruel: you, justice for my heartache
don't give.

(1321)

Listen, why to me do not you
pay attention…
your prisoner please listen to!
Pay attention!
Through the power you have you became rich:
such power made people to you
pay attention.
If one day some Persian lady did take your life,
then you'll of crown, status too,
pay attention?
You are the monarch now and you have power:
you can do anything, it is true?
Pay attention…
don't let the world trick you and don't be proud:
life has its ups and downs, if you
pay attention.
I put it all away… my heart, my life: I've ignored
it all in Mubariz's reign.* Please do
pay attention.

Jahan, in this world how much grief do you want?

You suffer much… to grief, you too

pay attention.

*Note: The dictator Mubariz Muzaffar who imprisoned Jahan. See Introduction.

(1325)

The One Who created me, my daily bread will give me...
the good days and bad are given to me by the Almighty.
The Creator created both bad and good, as He wished...
and I don't know a thing about what will be my destiny.
The Almighty created the stone for one to create the fire:
and gave the turquoise-colour as a gift to turquoise, see!
And the Creator created the beehive for all of the bees...
and the honey has many good uses for people, obviously.
The candle of all of the people full of misery has gone out:
their hearts are broken and we can't do anything, can we?
Poor heart of mine, why is it that you're suffering so much?
see the ants: out of the soil they can get their bread, daily.
Don't suffer in this world Jahan, the world is not worth it!
Why don't you do anything but keep on suffering, tell me!
Don't you know that you can't keep relying on the world...
because the world Jahan, will keep on deceiving, you see?

(1391)

O Allah, O my Lord, O my God, O Allah:
in the world, all under Your protection are!
All hearts full of faith are fresh and clean…
and all minds full of evil, from You are far.
You are God and to You we are obedient…
whatever You wish for us is good, O Allah!
All who are the enemy of You we will leave:
black from the white… always separated are!
I'm always remaining hopeful of Your grace:
sorry for all our faults we sincerely are, Allah!
O Jahan, O world, keep hoping to reach God:
if you want to win you should try even harder!

A SELECTION OF *RUBA'IS*

As a butterfly, to mate no one as faithful

is:

like butterfly, no one a friend, heart... full,

is.

A predatory enemy may kill a butterfly, but...

until it is dead, butterfly remaining faithful

is.

At morning I went into the garden full of pain,
and red rose told yellow about my pain, again.
Though far from me nightingale cries every day:
"Why your face yellow from pain's strain again?"

Flowers fade and to them we should bid goodbye,
or they can be completely left alone by you and I.
We should think deeply about both possibilities…
then let mind decide where the right way does lie.

I wonder... will the world ever be faithful one day?
I'm in pain... will you heal it, by coming this way?
What'll my life be in a day, a week or in a month?
What's Jahan to do, when world did it yesterday?

Don't worry, your heart the beloved will be reaching:
a day will finally come when my pain will be healing.
We should never be losing our hope or give up trying:
one day the night of separation will finally be ending.

There is someone who has your beautiful eyes…
and your beautiful face like the sun in the skies.
Last night I dreamt of the beautiful face of yours:
no better one than that one, in this dreamer lies!

O life, do not close your eyes on me so rudely…
don't laugh at vile feelings that come over me.
Open doors of happiness with your generosity:
open them for me, but close them for my enemy.

I had a fortunate destiny...

last night:

ah, you were mine, finally...

last night.

I dreamt I was biting your sweet lip...

I woke: bitten finger to see,

last night.

Look at the breeze, it wants to blow

again…

the garden of the world it put on show

again.

When I looked out at the flowers in the garden

I saw your face… lighting it with a glow

again.

In the fire in my heart I am burning:
poor me, all night I am not sleeping.
I am a lover in love with the beloved:
God, help… this problem be solving!

Everywhere I go I am thinking of you...
being away from you I am worried too.
Why am I not allowed to see your face...
how long should my heart wait for you?

I swore that him again I would never see:

deaf to temptations of sin... I'd be a Sufi!

Then I knew that it wasn't in my nature...

renunciations are now renounced, by me!

I've hidden your secrets in this heart

of mine:

from eyes, blood drops start to dart,

of mine.

For love of you I became the sacrificed lover...

beloved, to you it is a mere dying art

of mine!

Your handsome face is something I'll never deny!
That you're taller than a cypress will I ever deny?
You're so beautiful and shine like a large diamond,
O my beloved, your great beauty I can never deny!

How long should I wait to see your fair face?
I'm bewildered, looking for you in each place.
O beloved, the love of you makes me envious:
fair one, I look for you everywhere... no trace!

Suffering too much is this tired heart

of mine...

think about grief of heart kept apart...

of mine.

Please try to be kind and with your generosity,

begin to have some care for this heart

of mine.

Away from you, too much my suffering

comes:

I'm sad and world of Jahan, into grieving

comes.

This heart of mine has become like Layla's that

away from Majnun's... madness coming...

comes.

At all the ups and downs in the world I'm looking:
I see if someone isn't affected that one is winning.
But a person such as me is such a miserable wretch,
I will be with those with no home that all is losing.

O God, to have a lonely heart, do not let

me...

today don't allow such contempt to beset

me.

O azure wheel, for all others a easy horse you

provide to ride, but with a donkey you net

me!

Stand up, come to the garden, roses grow together:
not seeing Your face the nightingale grows quieter.
Why do You sting me, O You who are like a bee?
"With my kindness comes my sting," You answer.

My poor heart by destiny has been treated too unkindly,
in both worlds except for You no one else is kind to me.
I keep waiting and sitting here in the pathway of hope…
come to my rescue because no one else will… obviously!

I go here and there like a ball that someone else plays…
breath of patience with that One in me no longer stays.
Get up and come here, I can no longer endure separation;
hurry, for I've been waiting for days and days and days!

Every day you have a different way, a different manner:
the more I look at you the more I think you're even better.
I told myself to take you to court then perhaps I'd get my
heart back from you: but judge's heart you'd make flutter!

We have emptied many a full glass of the wine:
one more time I wish to bring your lips to mine.
Suddenly... I have felt a great fear for my life for
perhaps without our lips joined my life I'll resign.

Do you know that I am tulip-lean and liver-bloodied?
How much can I suffer? Hands off one so oppressed!
You stole my heart away then tossed it to the wind...
O my life and my world, stupidity's all I have gained!

O my friend, what happened? You never mention me?
By asking me to join you... you never make me happy.
Jahan's objective of being in this world is to join you...
so, why don't you answer this desire of mine... finally?

O source of my cure, you can't sit even one moment with one when by that one's face affliction is evident? If I am loving you with your Farhad-like ways do not blame me: you're sweet like Shirin and I'm indulgent.

The world mean, by being jealous of my peace of mind,

is…

if Jahan's in need of a drink the world drunk you'll find,

is.

But, I have no choice as this cycle takes so long to be

changing,

and it's tied my miserable hands and I know it unkind

is.

*Note: Notice the play on her name 'Jahan' that means
'the world'… she does this often.*

This is now spring, the time for flowers to grow:
the New Year is upon us… and this is so, it's so!
Be happy and don't worry in this old world of ours:
look at your life… it will go, before you even know.

In prison are all lovers that love you,

please come:

and they stay, yet you're unkind too...

please come.

You say that you are sorry for such cruel behaviour

but you know we'll be forgiving you...

please come.

The rose said, "In the world I'm the most beautiful, there is not a tulip that exists that is as colourful… I am not like the corn-poppy because that miserable flower with its heart that burns away, is so pitiful."

Late last night I woke my beloved and said this:
"I can't get to sleep all night, my mind on you is."
But now that today has finally come I regret this,
I dreamt this... and my understanding was amiss.

To the breeze this message was given by my heart:
"Please tell me... when we will no longer be apart?
Your eyes are large and shining, bright as the moon:
your hair's so beautiful it will surely trap my heart."

My loved one, calming my heart down

is:

they all tell me that he… an ugly clown

is.

He may not seem to be beautiful to others,

but to me he is and beside me lying down

is.

I'm sorry for all those ones who a friend,

have not:

they a friend to talk to and on to depend

have not.

They've no one to tell their grief to, so forgive these

sad people for except for me, they a friend

have not.

I feel sorry for anyone who from their home is

far away…

their friends and relatives they must miss…

far away.

They're like a prisoner locked up in an enemy's prison:

they're bored and sad for all dear to them is

far away.

I've nothing, no home, no heart, not a
world
throughout this kingdom of the Muzaffars.
Don't be deceived, O Jahan, by this
world…
one day's lucky, next unlucky, in this
world!

Nobody but the world, O Jahan... can wear us out:
each moment new thoughts, night new ideas sprout.
Don't be depending on the world for it is unfaithful:
each night it is in a different place, without a doubt.

O Lord, You forgive all of those who of sin are guilty,

You decorate the world with Your power, this I see…

I am here O Lord and I am crying in Your sight Lord,

come to my rescue, You own Jahan's world, and me!

The only opinion that we agree with is Your opinion;
no beautiful face but Yours, of them You are the one.
There is no asylum for me except that home of Yours:
everywhere can be seen Your slaves… by the million!

If only out of this sad place me You
should take…
and out of my heart this sorrow You
would take:
in this poor life of mine I have so many problems,
so You kindly away all my problems
should take.

Please, do not deprive me any longer of Your kindness,
don't give me anymore of this sea of sorrow, give less.
I no longer have a shelter left except for You I confess,
my hope is that You will not leave me… nevertheless!

Is there anything that the world does, except oppression?
It will grow a rose in ten days... only thorns from thereon.

It's an extremely difficult problem that is happening here:
we don't know what Fate does, when will it find solution?

Fate or Fortune... to whom, any attention will be paying?

To whom... will it some wealth and good luck be giving?

We cannot keep on trusting in the vicissitudes of time...

in whose way the thorn of oppression will it be placing?

The wealth that you have... my fortune

was not:

your pity to my poor heart... opportune

was not.

You know how favourable you were to my heart?

Like flower's life, it a week's honeymoon

was not.

Rose went, so we should now bid roses farewell:
from the world's people you should hide me well.
Corner with book and beloved and cup of wine:
that's what I deserve… I should do it for a spell.

His face from me that one keeps hiding,
every night with the others he is talking.
Sorrow of loving you I can't be leaving,
because to my heart it is still belonging!

O God, please look after me with Your generosity
for I am in Your sight with worship's foot to see…
and if You sell Joseph of Egypt inside my palace…
then I'm Egypt's Joseph and I'll buy You willingly.

O God... open Your door and poor me save,
and do not let me of any other be the slave:
I want to obey You and worship only You...
but how? I to any other worship never gave.

I have heard, that the police late last night
arrested a thief by using trickery, outright:
today as he was carried off he shouted out,
"Let me go… you tricked me, it's not right!"

O my Lord, O my God, O my Lord, O my God,

I don't know a way home except Your way God:

No one can hear my crying in both worlds Jahan,

no one can heal my pain except for One... God!

Please come back, with you bring happiness,

come:

I'm dying from these dreams of you: I stress,

come!

How much separation should I be in, in Ramadan?

Please, new moon bringing only happiness...

come!

Beloved, don't pay attention to me for only
one night;
that one only has not made me be happy…
one night.
If I should come to you and you won't open door to me
coming to you over your flat roof will be me
one night.

O God, please give to me the riches of insight, and please help obey You no matter my plight. When I am in a situation that is dangerous I'll try to think of You: help me with Your Might.

O my heart, of your beauty… proud

don't ever be;

be good, far from faith isn't allowed:

don't ever be!

O my heart, our doctor has no mercy for us at all…

sad about being far from the beloved,

don't ever be.

O God, firstly give to me the gift of belief:
I've pain… kindly heal me, give some relief.
I am so distressed… but I remain obedient:
calm my mind of all this distress and grief.

Just be careful of this world that is so horrible,
it changed my good nature to one despicable...
take a look at me today... tell me, what am I?
Where went when I was known as respectable?

Take as companion all those natural and saintly,
don't be their enemy because of another's policy.
If you wish to be companion of Prophet Solomon,
definitely the tormentor of any ant don't you be!

It's such a long time that I'm from You far away:

come…

although sorrowful I am hopeful faith will my way

come.

We have nothing to do with the world… have sat down:

we're poor… in dust of Your palace's floor we stay:

come!

O God, I am humbly praying, in Your sight I'm begging tonight:
it's time to pray silently for what from beloved I'm needing tonight.
Problem is heart and I want to get rid of my heart… because my heart keeps on continuing, in fire of love to be burning… tonight.

I have sacrificed my life for my beloved…

it's nothing:

from sorrow caused by that one I've bled:

it's nothing!

In this world I, a homeless one, don't suffer too much:

see how Jahan, from head to foot is dead:

it's nothing.

Sorrowfully, we keep dying... please a little healing send:

we have nothing but poverty... please a little caring send.

God... it has come to pass that this person is deadlocked:

God, for all our difficulties... please a little resolving send.

Back... the heart of our beloved,

we don't give:

beloved's heart to others instead,

we don't give.

I'm in love with your face and my heart is like a

valuable pearl and to a deadhead

we don't give.

From these times that are passing,

we can't escape;

from world that is us oppressing,

we can't escape.

This oppression of this world is a much easier thing

than ones offensive to be escaping.

We can't escape!

You come... Your kindness and generosity
I see:
when You come, a peace in this mind of me,
I see.
When You are hidden, then I see You everywhere:
everywhere I keep looking... You constantly
I see.

Look at these two roses... O you Persian moon:
one day one like gold, other like firewood soon.
They are like two lovers that have sat together:
one shame made red, one grief... yellow, moon!

O God, please forgive me with Your generosity...
O God, please don't stop paying attention to me.
Who am I, and who will take my name with him?
If I sin be generous, kindly forgive Your devotee.

With world's grief don't be sympathetic,

my heart;

when beloved is away don't be heartsick,

my heart:

If other people should give you advice be careful…

listen to your friend, "It may be a trick,

my heart."

O world, why don't you ever agree

with the people:

why can't you be honest, tell me…

with the people?

Until Jahan was alive in the world no one heard that

by the world was done this jugglery

with the people.

Shiraz is really wonderful... but especially in spring when by river the beloved's with you, wine drinking; listening to harp, *daf, kamancheh* and aloes wood... and all of this with your sweetheart who is so loving.

There's one who's an equal to that One? There
is not?
In my world a one as wise as You, anywhere...
is not!
All of us are so weak and we are so small just like ants;
as one existing as powerful as You, I declare ...
"Is not!"

This world, Jahan, is really just like a toy… a plaything:
each moment's different, something special's happening.
O little heart of mine when you play you must be careful,
because in beloved's way there are many secrets waiting.

Growing up in the garden every kind of

flower is:

emerald in desert, plain and valley to

discover is.

Take up that cup of yours and come slowly to me:

come, now the time for drinking wine

together is.

TARJI BAND (strophe poem)

In my life to come, to get You is now my only aim:
whenever I see Your face I get younger… I claim.
You should be kind to such poor people, like me…
if You can do it, do it now… and there's no blame.
If You continue to avoid me for any longer… then
I will follow wherever You go… like a heavy chain.
The Angel of the Invisible World now tells me…
in language that is silent, that one did proclaim:
"Withdraw from all the people in the world Jahan
if to One with a beautiful face your love you aim."
I'll give everything that I have if You come to me,
in Jahan's world You're the investment I acclaim.
I have lost all patience from being far from You…
O so miserable and so sick and so tired I became!
All I am wishing is that I can soon come to You…
perhaps one day You will pay attention to me too!

Love is eternal and it will keep going for eternity…
love will change people and will stay… a certainty.
Love's like a mirror in which we can see the world,
in it is seen both the good and the bad… you see?
It is the truth that every person will be loving You,
if all of them are intelligent, and fully aware they be.
To look at You is not allowed in the religion of one
who thinks of herself and about herself does worry.
My heart is sick and tired because of my Beloved:
none can reach, none can touch the Beloved of me.
I love You… yet can't find myself at this moment:
when will I be able to find me… myself, really be?
All I am wishing is that I can soon come to You…
perhaps one day You will pay attention to me too!

You're the direction where Jahan prays continually:
all people worship You knowingly or unknowingly.
Yet You've withdrawn from all the world's people,
and now You are existing in the Beyond obviously.
To me the soft breeze a scent of You has brought…
and it smells so good that it smells divine… to me.
It is Your desire that only Justice will be prevailing:
it's also Your wish that only the good for me will be.
You are the Spirit in all of us and we are all the form:
You are the Mind in us and we are skin on the body.
It is not only now that I have been worshipping You:
for such a long time You've been worshipped by me.
It's for the better part of a century… this worship by
me of You: for a long time in my mind, completely.
All I am wishing is that I can soon come to You…
perhaps one day You will pay attention to me too!

O Winebringer... a glass of wine to me be bringing:
come and heal this sick heart of mine... I am tiring!
It is true that old age is finally catching up with me,
so give me a glass of wine and me young be making.
O you Minstrel... come and play and earn your pay:
play on the harp and also the *ney's* reed be blowing.
I feel like I'm beginning to die from the love of You:
one day to Your lover... some attention be paying.
O dear companion of the mind of this one so lonely
have some pity on us for we're alone and weeping.
Breeze, when you go and finally reach my Beloved,
to that One quickly of my great desire be telling...
tell that One, "Why think only of the reward in the
other world? Of this world and of Jahan be caring."
All I am wishing is that I can soon come to You...
perhaps one day You will pay attention to me too!

One day it happened... my life completely changed:
I had no money or position, my life was rearranged.
Before this occurred towards people I was pleasant,
I was happy and before me my destiny was spread.
Slaves were many waiting on my every command...
beautiful slaves with smooth bodies... so easily led.
If those slaves weren't ordered by me to do anything
they remained still, doing nothing unless I ordered.
Now that I'm in love with You, every day and every
night, week, month, year... by me You are praised.
In Your Love I'm burning, I burn away: I burn away
my mind as imagination to my Spiritual Self is led.
Because of the love of You I'm now one who is sick;
everywhere and all ways this one has been affected.
All I am wishing is that I can soon come to You...
perhaps one day You will pay attention to me too!

I wake for You! Want to sleep? I think of Your hair!
Separation breaks heart like stone on glass, I swear!
Come back, O come back to me, for being far away
from You all patience has disappeared into thin air.
Because of my wretched body... soul feels distressed
and because of sorrowful soul my body doesn't care.
Everyday I'm suffering because of this love of You...
I suffer much being away from You, come back here.
Everywhere I was traveling I kept searching for You:
yes I was, during every day, every year, everywhere.
Everywhere I looked I was unable to discover You...
in this desperate endeavour success was... nowhere!
All I am wishing is that I can soon come to You...
perhaps one day You will pay attention to me too!

O You Who are my Beloved, You Who I'm loving,
O You Who are the One, Who me safe is keeping:
it should be known by You… for such a long time
I've loved You… in Your Love let me keep staying.
Please… please be kind to me, Your faithful lover:
as You are my Friend, Your friend You be helping.
True… everything and everyone else I've forgotten:
but me forgetting You is truly an impossible thing.
I've been preached at by everyone about Your Love:
it's possible that Your Love anyone can be avoiding?
It is not possible for me to avoid worshipping You…
I'll worship You, Beloved, until I'm no longer living.
All I am wishing is that I can soon come to You…
perhaps one day You will pay attention to me too!

ELEGY POEMS:

(Marsie)

for Soltan Bakht (her daughter).

O how I regret that I've lost my darling daughter…
my dear daughter's dead, so young when I lost her.
So kind… a face like the moon… but what can I do?
All patience I've lost… kept from her, as a prisoner.
now the nightingale's song isn't heard in a garden:
my beautiful girl cut from the garden, like a flower.
O heart, when will you go to the house where she is?
She left me: with the caravan has gone my daughter.
I cried out so loud even the sky heard my complaint:
tears ran deep… like rain down drainpipe they were.
She was always a girl who had a happy disposition:
why did she die? Did my bad luck transfer onto her?
Darling, Jahan's world was destroyed when you left:
you left a world and Jahan, when you so young were.
She took grief and happiness from the world, Jahan…
she passed away, now of world Jahan is relinquisher.

O my darling, heart and eyes too much are suffering...
I suffer more when these feelings I try to be explaining.
Because of this world my tearful eyes continue to weep:
now missing you... like Jehun River, tears keep flowing.
When I finally was able to see my friends they all said:
"Poor woman, can this situation cause more suffering?"
How can I ever tell how much I have suffered from this?
All should be aware it's more than I can ever be telling!
I continue to complain about this cruel world... because
her beautiful, young face now under the dust is hiding.
I'll cry so much, being far from your beautiful face, that
from my heart all of its red blood will be soon leaving.
Tell me, O where does the heart of my Layla now go?
Jahan is like Majnun, made mad by her disappearing!
O my dear heart, your sweet life has now finished and
there is nothing left for us... but to continue suffering.

Rose fell and hid herself from the world's garden:
she caused nightingale's love to be weary, broken.
No more smiling rose in my garden of oppression:
hope I had was lost, and patience I have forsaken.
When you left my fate changed… I was unlucky:
being far from you made me homeless once again.
It was not my fortune to eventually come to you:
my misfortune has made it a night of separation.
Only one way it can be described… unfortunate.
From flower one can hide sunshine: where, when?
I shout at the heavens… what else can I do now?
What can I do but try to be patient, try, try again.
My grief from being far from you is such, doctors
can't heal this heart of mine that is in such pain.

I've suffered much too much in this world Jahan…
but with the Lord's help some peace I will obtain.
I suffered so much because of losing many friends:
when I finally lost *you* I became broken… insane.

Separated from you makes me burn away in a fire:
I cry again and my tears make the rivers rise higher.
I'll do nothing but complain about this cruel world:
from it Jahan has a life thrown upon a funeral pyre.
I swear on dust of my darling, dear daughter, that
ever since long ago… back then when I was born I
have seen in this world only unkindness and much
cruelty and in my life I've found nothing to satisfy.
This world's taken all of my patience from me and
given back to me nothing but suffering and desire.
There's been too much suffering in world of Jahan:
and from the people I now see only pain I acquire.
Each man I fell in love with has broken my heart…
I'd hopes, but they kept secrets when I did inquire.
What can I keep on saying of what happens to me?
Tell to me this: who has a life like mine? Sir, sire?
The wind blew up and my flower was destroyed…
patience left, soul from grief's thorn, began to tire.
Who created me to be having such a… terrible fate?
Who has destroyed my life, by lighting grief's fire?
O my darling, my sweet heart… my Soltan Bakht,
none are like you… only to see your face, I desire.

When she left us, the world and Jahan suffered so
much we wept: she bid me farewell then did expire.
World and Jahan is envious of her... for in the dust
she is placed to stay forever... my poor daughter,
I regret that in this world you had not a happy time
and suffering in your mind... is all you did acquire.
She didn't experience much kindness in this world,
she did not have one evil thought or selfish desire.
What a destiny! A fortune that couldn't be worse!
Nothing from Jahan and this world but grief's fire!
I was never allowed to see you shining like the sun:
of my broken heart you weren't let to kindly inquire.

God the Almighty causes narcissus to be growing,
and God destroyed it... with the scythe of grieving.
It's the Almighty Who causes the cypress to grow,
and it is God's wrath that causes it to be yielding.
Doctor who advises me and my companions say...
"Keep being patient... the only way to keep going."
I heard a voice: "O nightingale of love when world,
Jahan, takes your flower, what's gained by crying?"
Whatever God wants us to do we will be obedient:
please God, me to be more patient keep on helping.
God, he took my daughter from me in my torment:
"Farewell" to my home of happiness, I was saying.
And if I happen to cry out loudly like the harp and
if from grieving like the aloes wood I am burning...
you are right to give what I have, You're my Lord
to obey and satisfy: all You ask I'll be sacrificing.
It is true for one to say that somebody now has died:
it is true... God one from another has been parting.
If You need set one aside for sacrifice I offer myself:
if You want to destroy one... Jahan's life be taking.
Please show Your kindness and give forgiveness...
though I lost hope such fortune I'll ever be having.

This injured heart continues to find fault with me,

all I can hope is that more fortunate is my ending.

I know I haven't been always good, but with Your

kindness not being a failure in Your eyes I'm hoping.

If You do not give what Jahan desires in this world

it's not important, to reach You is all I'm wanting.

O rose, my flower, you who are my garden's cypress.
My little bud, my fruit, my love how can I express?
O my poor daughter, poor broken heart's daughter,
whose death at a young age causes such distress...
my eyes won't see that beautiful young face again:
that one's now hidden like sea's mermaid-princess.
If I should cry don't criticize because from being far
from Joseph, Jacob cried each day from his distress.
What wound do I have that there's no ointment for?
What pain have I, that only crying eases my stress?
Every time a tear of mine drops like rain in the earth
one finds a pearl worth more than Oman's: no less!
While I'm still alive and still have eyes and a mouth
I'll not forget her name, beautiful eyes loving caress.
My heart has been burnt so much that if I should die
you would never be able to find it among my ashes.
One time my house seemed to be just like a heaven;
now it's dark as this prison holding only loneliness.
Now, I don't have any guest except for my grieving,
when once house of my heart was full of happiness.
I'm beginning to wonder if I should lose my patience
again: this ship again saves one drowning: no... yes?

Go from this place for a few days when it is autumn:
the nightingale must leave a garden for a wilderness.
If we have to keep going on living, this is my destiny:
I shouldn't complain of unhappy days, of more or less.

There is a pain in the world Jahan's not experienced
and some grief the rotten world to Jahan has not fed?
Is there an oppression or regret that I have not seen
that cruelly caused my face to turn red, bloody red?
Is there a cypress not passing away before my eyes,
that had not made from my eyes blood to have bled?
What fault have I or have I done, to be punished so?
Perhaps my destiny is bad luck, or a destiny misled.
My beautiful Layla has been taken from my sight…
I am like Majnun, who from her loss… lost his head.
When snake of separation strikes and my heart hurts,
do not think it will by a thousand charms be healed.
Fire burning in my heart will be calmed by my tears,
but after some time passes it will rage… will spread.
If any one looks at my face you'll easily see my tears
but you'll not know my heartburn, better left unsaid.
Jahan was burnt by grief but of all hearts in the world
who can be patient with her in her grief: enough said?
God, answer me… there's no one else like me I know:
who with this fate, O beloved, weakness by sin is led.
But… I still live, hoping God will forgive my mistakes
and bring me out safely from hell's fire and this dread.

O God, please open up one of the doors of Your heaven for my fairy-like daughter: please, I ask you once again. Please, find a place in heaven for my fairy-like daughter: give a place to her, so that Your angel may sit with her. Please help her so that she can avoid those of this world: please help her, so from her soul a light may be unfurled.

This world that is base took her with her high spirit…
it was her kindness that made her for Your heaven fit.
Don't put the flower in dust of grave of my daughter:
my chaste daughter to highest heaven, take, forever.
Please help her forget the world, Jahan's world also…
ambergris, musk's scent and joy into her heart blow!

This misfortune of mine… God has given this to me:
O God, I do not wish anyone else has such a destiny.
Yes… I cannot stop weeping and I keep saying to all,
"O my companions… my Soltan Bakht is lost to me."

If God has closed one door to her in this world, Jahan;

even though a thorn should become a pain in her leg…

it is not a guess I have but I can assure you I'm certain

that my dear daughter's with an angel now in heaven.

The arrow of separation from you has now killed me…
my heart, it was like a strong shield… now dead it be:
The doctor saw how mortally I was wounded and said:
"What's wrong here can't be healed, an impossibility!"

O world, how much misfortune do you want for Jahan?
O my tired heart, of me you should be shy… if you can:
my life is in no way like the life I had desired it to be…
and what I got gave no good since my bad luck began.

That one was like a painting full of color, full of beauty:

that one, she had a cheek like a tulip, delightful to see.

All desire that Jahan has for the world has disappeared,

that one... was hidden from the world's people and me.

Does the world want to sew for me a cloak of grieving? Look closely at me, you'll see that my heart's burning: my heart that keeps burning may be a secret you don't know, but I see it clearly... burning, burning, burning!

In spite of the fact that the world to me was no good,

and flower of garden of my heart took when it could,

I still saw with my own eyes that God with kindness

opened a door of heaven to her… as that One should.

It was so… whenever I saw a flower I was cheered up,
I was as happy as when with her I'd drink love's cup;
but I could not smell her fragrance ever again because
the world took it from Jahan: I was made to give it up!

It developed so that she became suddenly scared of me,
I was told that it was her choice to be away… you see?
And then it became this… no attention to me she paid:
mournful sigh of her mother she didn't hear, obviously.

When you no longer saw me, on my honour this I swear...
the patience that I'd borne before I could no longer bear.
O my darling, for how much longer will you be sleeping?
O Jahan's world, wake one more time, wake up my dear!

Although the world lied to kings and took their lives too;
kings of the world, Jahan, still desire the world… it's true!
Soltan Bakht's death has killed this world and me, Jahan:
heart of the world of Jahan is burnt up, this one can't undo.

I couldn't sleep for even a moment being far away from her,

and all happening in Jahan's world wasn't peaceful either;

then all of a sudden I'm informed that my daughter's dead:

in Jahan's world I've only now… her, away so much further.

Being far from you my heart has become like a loaf of bread:
my eyes instead of weeping tears keep weeping only blood.
Because I keep being so far away from your beautiful face…
my face from my weeping blood had eventually turned red.

: *QIT'AS* (Fragments)

O you dear happy man... may happiness be here, with you!
On this New Year's Day... may you only in happiness be!
O dear man, who can cause happiness to be lasting forever,
my wish is... only what is good for you, this... I stress, BE!
The humblest slave of yours is Jamshid the mighty king and
may the least of your servants King Feridun, (none less) be!
May you get everything you wish from the world and Jahan,
and may your Friend Almighty God, Who is matchless, be!
Any person who is not happy about you being our monarch,
may that particular person's mind forever full of sadness be!
And any person who isn't honourable in this Court of yours,
his eyes bleeding like a Jehun River that is bottomless... be!
And if a person may feel anything but kindness towards you,
may pleasure of that one like a loaf of bread... or even less be.
And may far away from you be forever sadness and grieving,
may your life be long and your royalty in everlastingness be!
World of Jahan is brought down by people of the lowest kind:
dust in the eyes, of those people that me try to depress... be!
There's one who has filled my eyes with the tears of grieving:
that one's heart full of Jahan's and world's grief, no less... be!

May that one's star of fortune and that one's luck luckless
be,
may that one's fate be fateful, his pleasure lacking success
be!
New Year's Day and week and year, month and every day
raining on our king's reign and inside our king… happiness
be!
And may doors of all happiness and those of every pleasure
be opened up to him and shut on that one's enemies' success
be.
Naushiravan, Kai Khusrau and Gaghfour and Kai Kobad,
all long ago, the dust of your royal throne also their address
be.
If a person should disobey your orders then like blow of a lion
may that one's back broken by a disastrous blow's caress…
be!

I said to grief... "Of my friends in the world,
no one keeps remaining as faithful, as you."
Grief said, "What do you expect, being alone:
you can keep on living without a friend too?"
It is true that anybody can win this game, if
with grief that person is completely through.
Be happy and do not worry at all about grief...
Rustom, Kai Kaus, on earth what did they do?
My eyes weep blood instead of tears from grief:
washing tears off faces... but friend, not off you.

Though it's possible for my friend to be doing it,
kindly paying any attention to me, he does not!
Why keep filling enemy's heart with happiness
and continue tying this friend's heart in a knot?
Don't, for in the garden of heart of those faithful
somebody picking up the tree of kindness is not.

Last night in a dream my eyes saw good fortune...
the garden of my hope was decorated beautifully:
Jahan's world was full of tulips and happiness and
beside me sat beloved, our enemy we couldn't see.
The full moon was out for me... my heart was light
although it'd been waned of moon that was lucky.
I whispered, "Thank you God!" Then I said, "At
least I've finally had everything I wished, for me!"

How pleasant is telling jokes and to good friends talking,

hearing *daf* and *kamancheh* as our way into desert wends,

and if my beloved comes over to be with me it is so good…

I'll do all I can to make sure time with me that one spends.

If somebody is imprisoned by the world, Jahan...

the people begin to, about how he is feeling,

ask:

but if someone calls out *my* name by a mistake,

thousand times he'll for forgiveness, fearing

ask!

I live in a corner of a school older than my heart:
I have been sitting here as alone as any dervish!
I don't live in safety from the world's big mouth,
thinking deeply about my fate isn't being selfish.
My heart seems always full of blood because *they*
keep pushing fingers into my sore that's feverish.
I've no interest in position or wealth in this world:
I'm one who remains contented by my will's wish.
I do not know what they want of me, I'm so tired:
they'll gossip about me even if I do as they wish.

My sweetheart, I expected you to be more kind to me:

in the world Jahan chose you, you are mine, I thought!

From my garden of hope for you a thorn was my share,

so I was disappointed and I left the garden distraught.

Is there a kind of kindness God has withheld from me?
If I could, in a thousand languages I'd be appreciative!
I remember that One in my heart, every day and night;
if I didn't I would hate it, leave it and it... not forgive!
When I'm looking at everything, I'm seeing only God:
my greatest wish is for whatever God, will me... give!

With justice that you have in this world of Jahan,
between wolf and the lamb... there is some peace?
Can it be called justice... when inside of my heart
you laid grief and sadness down, with no release?
You don't ever ask of yourself why... why did you
take away everything that was for my happiness?
You say you're happy with *some* people's marriage:
but you left me in nothing but grief's separateness.

Can you believe I continue to accept whatever life
has given to me? That's all I ever had to possess!

Although not any power in the world have I, Jahan;
I prefer power of that One, of all the world's power:
if all in the world is in some danger from that storm,
Noah's with us... the sea we should never empower!

"To penetrate into the essence of all being and significance
and to release the fragrance of that inner attainment
for the guidance and benefit of others, by expressing
in the world of forms, truth, love, purity and beauty...
this is the only game which has any intrinsic and absolute
worth. All other, happenings, incidents and attainments can,
in themselves, have no lasting importance."
Meher Baba

Printed by Amazon Italia Logistica S.r.l.
Torrazza Piemonte (TO), Italy